P9-DDP-491

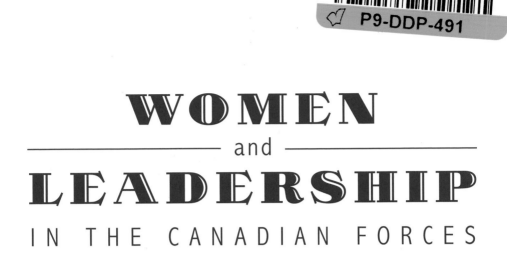

WOMEN
and
LEADERSHIP
IN THE CANADIAN FORCES

WOMEN AND LEADERSHIP IN THE CANADIAN FORCES:

PERSPECTIVES AND EXPERIENCE

Edited by:
Karen D. Davis

CANADIAN DEFENCE ACADEMY PRESS

Copyright © 2009 Her Majesty the Queen in Right of Canada, as represented by the Minister of National Defence.

Canadian Defence Academy Press
PO Box 17000 Stn Forces
Kingston, Ontario   K7K 7B4

Produced for the Canadian Defence Academy Press
by 17 Wing Winnipeg Publishing Office.
WPO30287

Front Cover Photos: Provided by Canadian Forces Combat Camera
Back Cover Photo: Petty Officer 2nd Class Ivan Lightwood

Library and Archives Canada Cataloguing in Publication

Davis, Karen D. (Karen Dianne), 1956-
Women and leadership in the Canadian Forces : perspectives and experience /
edited by Karen D. Davis.

Issued by Canadian Defence Academy.
Includes bibliographical references.
ISBN 978-0-662-46296-5 (bound).--ISBN 978-0-662-46297-2 (pbk.)
Cat. no.: D2-210/1-2007E (bound).-- Cat. no.: D2-210/2-2007E (pbk.)

1. Canada--Armed Forces--Women. 2. Command of troops. 3. Women and the military--Canada. 4. Women soldiers--Canada. 5. Canada--Armed Forces. I. Canadian Defence Academy II. Title.

UB419.C3D38 2008   355.0082'0971   C2007-980286-9

Printed in Canada.

3 5 7 9 10 8 6 4

**For all the women and men of
5 Area Support Group**

Land Force Quebec Area

In memory of your commander (2007-2008),
Colonel Karen Ritchie, OMM, CD
1963 - 2008

In Memory of

Chief Petty Officer 2nd Class Deborah Ann Andrews
1952 - 1997

&

Captain Nichola Kathleen Sarah Goddard
1980 - 2006

ACKNOWLEDGEMENTS

A special thank you to the contributors to this volume. You have generously shared your knowledge and experience, thus exemplifying an important responsibility of leadership – contribution to the professional development of others. Also, my sincere gratitude is extended to each of you for the confidence and trust that you have placed in me through your commitment to this book. It has been inspiring to work with you, and just as I have, many others will learn from your example.

The opportunity to produce a volume such as this is rare. The end product represents the effort, time, commitment, abilities, guidance, and leadership of many. In particular, the opportunity, leadership, and coaching provided by Colonel Bernd Horn, the Director of the Canadian Forces Leadership Institute, made this volume possible. His expertise, insight, and skill as a writer and editor, along with his commitment and encouragement, ensured that an idea became a reality.

A sincere thank you is extended to Mélanie Denis for her enthusiasm, creativity, expertise, judgment, and assistance with photos and design elements of this book. Appreciation is also extended to Dr. Phyllis Browne and Justin Wright for their expert and timely review of some of the material.

I would certainly be remiss if I did not acknowledge the meticulous attention to detail and expertise that was applied to both the copy-edit process and the final design of this volume by Captain Phil Dawes and his staff at the 17 Wing Publishing Office. Thank you for your outstanding contribution to the final product.

TABLE OF CONTENTS

FOREWORD

It gives me great pleasure to introduce this unique leadership volume, *Women and Leadership in the Canadian Forces: Perspectives and Experience*, the first book to come off the Canadian Defence Academy press that focuses exclusively on the contemporary leadership experiences of women in the Canadian Forces. The contributors to this book share success as leaders in the Canadian Forces as well as a commitment to passing on their triumphs and lessons-learned in the hope that others will benefit. The volume spans the last three decades of women's contributions and thus puts a spotlight on the growing opportunities for women to serve and lead in the Canadian Forces. It highlights the enthusiasm with which women have embraced the opportunities, and excelled in spite of the obstacles encountered along the way. Importantly, several chapters in the book also offer insight into some of the social, psychological and organizational processes that are relevant to the experience of women and men in the Canadian military today.

I expect that some will question the publication of a volume that includes only the experiences of women. After all, gender integration has been considered, by many, to be complete since the end of the 10-year period spanning 1989-1999, when, as a result of the 1989 Canadian Human Rights Tribunal direction, the Canadian Forces was closely monitored in its activities related to the employment of women. The material presented in this volume illustrates the significant capabilities and contributions that women bring to the Canadian Forces; however, it also serves as a caution against taking the current status of women in the Canadian Forces for granted. The experiences of the contributors underscore some of the challenges that persist even though "gender integration" has come a very long way.

For several decades, many have understood the importance of accessing a full range of opportunities for women to contribute to the Canadian military, and as such have contributed countless hours preparing briefings, appearing before committees, participating in organizations such as the Association for Women's Equity in the Canadian Forces and as members of initiatives such as the Minister's Advisory Board on Gender Integration. This volume provides powerful testimony to the vision that many of us worked toward throughout the 1970s, 80s, and 90s.

This volume also profiles perspectives and voices that have been largely invisible within the professional development culture of the Canadian Forces, and as such is long overdue. The success of the Canadian Forces is dependent upon all of its leaders, and the organization can ill afford to exclude the contributions of any of them. Through the leadership experiences shared in this book, those with similar experiences or facing parallel challenges can move forward with increased confidence in their capacity to lead, and those with very different experiences can enhance their ability to lead diverse teams facing diverse challenges. Thus, this volume begins to address a gap that represents a call to all leaders in the Canadian Forces to ensure that they share their perspective and experiences so that others may become better prepared to meet the challenges of the future.

The Canadian Forces thrives on the contributions of many gifted leaders, including those who have shared their experiences in *Women and Leadership in the Canadian Forces: Perspectives and Experience* – an important resource for all who are committed to increasing their knowledge and developing their capacity to lead in the future.

Sheila Hellstrom, CD
Brigadier-General (retired)

March 2007

PREFACE

The Canadian Forces Leadership Institute (CFLI) is proud to release this latest book *Women and Leadership in the Canadian Forces: Perspectives and Experience*. This is the first time that the Canadian Defence Academy Press has published a book exclusive on the experience of women. The editor, Lieutenant-Commander (retired) Karen Davis, has assembled the experiences of a number of women who have served in operational roles as well as several research papers that lend a collective voice to some of the triumphs and challenges that have been faced by women in the Canadian Forces. The integration of research and experience into one volume provides the reader with insight into both the practical experience of leadership, and the social processes that influence that experience.

This volume, through its exclusive focus on the experiences of women, addresses an important aspect of the current and future leadership of the Canadian Forces. The experience of women in the Canadian Forces is in many ways the same as that of their male peers; however, it is also unique from that of men in some ways and at some times. Such an acknowledgement in no way undermines the significance of the shared responsibilities and challenges that Canadian Forces members, male and female, confront as leaders and as teams. The voices that have contributed to this volume agree, without exception, that they joined the military to be part of the team, serve the people of Canada, and share experiences with others, regardless of gender. However, in achieving this shared experience they have had to reconcile and manage the fact that they are women, in various ways. The volume represents a valuable resource for servicewomen who are developing their leadership acumen, as well as those leaders, male and female, who are leading increasingly diverse teams that include women and men from all corners and cultures of Canadian society.

In closing, I wish to reiterate the importance of this volume. The information contained herein provides insight, ideas and knowledge that impact leadership and the profession of arms. As such, all military members have a responsibility to ensure they continue to develop professionally through education, training, experience and self-development. As always, we welcome your feedback and comments.

Bernd Horn

Colonel

Director, CFLI

INTRODUCTION

Karen D. Davis

Regardless of their occupation, women serve in all environments in the CF, and thus are employed in a substantial range of operational and leadership roles, including in overseas operational theatres such as Afghanistan. Representation, while somewhat low at 13 percent of Regular Force and 20 percent of Reserve Force CF members, has increased steadily in recent decades. *Women and Leadership in the Canadian Forces: Perspectives and Experience*, exactly as the title suggests, showcases incredible experience, interesting perspectives, and valuable insights from women who have proven abilities and achievements as leaders in the CF.

Much of what we have heard about women in the CF over the past 30 years has been in reference to the barriers they have faced, the harassment that has plagued their experience, and the doubts that have been expressed about their ability to perform in a full range of military roles. All too often, misperceptions have persisted in regard to issues such as the suitability of women to the rigours of ground combat, the impact of women and men in close proximity away from home, the effectiveness of mixed male/female combat units, the motivation of women to serve in combat units, and the impact of bearing and raising children on women's readiness to deploy.[1] In fact, the citation below is an excerpt from an editorial that appeared in the *National Post* in November 2005:

> The military is – was – a unique, genetics-dependent culture, as specific to males as midwifery is to females. Males don't fight for the feminist ideal of androgyny, but to protect the women they love – wives, daughters, mothers, sisters – and the values they represent – normalcy, freedom and peace...Apart from rear-service, medical and administrative functions, where they shine, women don't belong in the CF.[2]

This could easily be mistaken for something written circa World War II! The editorial resulted in a flurry of response, by both women and men in the CF, challenging this dogma. While ridiculous on the one hand, the editorial is also useful in rendering very visible the underlying values and assumptions informing beliefs regarding the suitability of women in a full range of military roles. The leadership experiences of the women who have contributed to this volume are exemplary in challenging these misperceptions.

This book provides an opportunity for readers to learn from women who have successfully negotiated various challenges, often with the exceptional support of male team members, peers and leaders, to become competent, committed, and professional leaders in a broad range of operational roles. Most acknowledge that, for the most part, their experience has not focused on the fact that they are women, but on developing their technical expertise and being the best serviceperson and leader that they can be. However, without exception, they have had to reconcile and negotiate experiences that are unique from their male peers, based on the fact that they are women.

The initial approach to this volume was based upon the knowledge that women in the CF are accumulating significant leadership experience, but still isolated enough in some domains that individual women and men often do not have the opportunity to benefit from the unique lessons learned of women who have both operational and leadership experience. For example, although women now represent approximately 9.6 percent of the Regular Force senior officer corps, at the time of writing there are only four female generals (all at the Brigadier-General/Commodore rank) and 13 full colonels serving, and most of these senior women are in National Defence Headquarters in Ottawa. One notable exception is recently promoted Brigadier-General Christine Whitecross, who is the Commander of Joint Task Force North, headquartered in Yellowknife, Northwest Territories. As such, the contributors were asked to consider their leadership experience from their perspective as women in the CF, and in particular in operational environments. In addition to personal experience, several authors offer leadership and research perspectives on issues impacting women and leadership in the CF. The integration of various perspectives into one volume provides a one-stop resource of personal accounts that go beyond the available research on women and leadership in the military. The perspectives and research, provided in the last four chapters, both inform and reinforce the leadership experiences presented earlier in the volume.

Leadership can be interpreted in many ways. Thus, it is important to clarify the CF perspective on leadership that, in one way or another, influences all who serve. All members of the CF, regardless of rank or position, are expected to develop their leadership ability and can be called upon to exercise leadership in any given situation. CF doctrine defines leadership in terms of personal attributes or position as "directly or indirectly influencing others, by means of formal authority or personal attributes, to act in accordance with one's intent or a shared purpose".[3] *Effective leadership* is defined as "directing, motivating, and enabling others to accomplish the mission professionally and ethically, while developing or improving capabilities that contribute to mission success".[4] In addition, leadership doctrine emphasizes that the effectiveness of the CF depends upon a strong officer/non-commissioned member leadership team that shares responsibility, identity, values, and purpose.

The leaders that have contributed to this volume reinforce this doctrine in numerous ways, including personal example and commitment to their team and the CF mission. The result is a collection of insights that both reflect, and contribute to, the developing maturity of the CF and its leaders as a gender integrated organization.

In chapter 1, Major Anne Reiffenstein challenges the organization to take a close look at what gender integration means and how and where the CF has achieved it. Her experience and success, along with that of her fallen artillery comrade, Captain Nichola Goddard, provides powerful testimony to the contribution that women have made to the CF. However, as Major Reiffenstein's experience highlights, there are numerous issues that continue to impact the experience of women as they strive to develop permanent status in previously uncharted domains. One of the key challenges is the continuing isolation that female leaders face in operational environments. For individual soldiers, this can result in social isolation, but also means that they are constantly addressing similar issues over and over again as they continuously find themselves in different units and organizations that do not have, and may not have ever had, any women at all. A woman in such a position becomes fully responsible for developing the strategies and processes that she will need to effectively negotiate her leadership role and career development when there is no one with whom to share similar experiences and to learn from.

In chapter 2, Commodore Margaret Kavanagh shares several milestones over her 30-year career in the CF, exemplified by both challenge and opportunity. As we hear more and more about the need for adaptability in the changing security environment, Commodore Kavanagh's experience provides numerous examples of the ways in which adaptability in response to CF policies, in reference to the employment of women in particular, allowed her to develop a rewarding and successful career. Career planning is important, but it is imperative that any CF member, including women, be prepared to take advantage of opportunities as they present themselves.

During her time in the military, Major (retired) Sue Forgues experienced more combat action than most, if not all, of her Canadian peers at the time. In chapter 3, she offers a unique glimpse into her experience as a Canadian tactical helicopter pilot, deployed on numerous missions with the Royal Air Force while on an exchange posting in the United Kingdom. She was challenged not only by the intensity of operations that she experienced, but also as a Canadian female pilot serving with an air force that had only recently trained its first female helicopter pilot. Major Forgues shares her strategies for negotiating unique leadership challenges, both as a female leader in a male domain, but also as a Canadian officer responsible for the lives of aircrew from another nation.

Until 2003, a female had never commanded a Canadian naval warship. Carefully considering the potential impact of her notoriety on her crew, in chapter 4 Lieutenant-Commander Marta Mulkins provides a candid description of the way that she approached her leadership responsibilities as the first female commander of a Canadian naval warship. Importantly, she acknowledges the full and immediate support of her command team, the executive officer and the coxswain, whom she knew would have a significant influence on the crew's confidence in her leadership. Understanding that the key to her ship's success would be the discipline, professionalism and expertise of her crew, she strove to reinforce a military ethos that was fair, yet uncompromising when it came to commitment and hard work. She focused on her crew, while ensuring that the attention that she received as a female commander was managed as a minor inconvenience rather than taking any priority over her crew's achievements.

As a female tactical helicopter pilot, Major Jamie Speiser-Blanchet knows that being a woman has frequently put her under a spotlight. In chapter 5, she acknowledges that in the early days of her career she may have modified her behaviour to avoid undue attention as a female, but describes how she quickly recognized that she could either accept the attention and learn to coexist with it peacefully, or she could let it eat at her and slowly erode her self-confidence and peace of mind. Today, Major Speiser-Blanchet has let go of any preconceived notions about what others may think of her. Her leadership strategy places a high emphasis on learning from others, open feedback and communication, sharing experiences, and transparency in her approach to subordinates, peers, and superiors. Although she acknowledges that perfection is not realistic, her tendency to be a perfectionist, along with her aversion to failure, does contribute to her will to succeed.

In chapter 6, Major Deanna Manson moves away from a personal focus to profile the achievements and contributions of women in the Traffic Technician trade in the CF. The Traffic Technician trade was opened to women in 1976, although at that time their employment was limited to administrative functions such as furniture and effects clerks, shipping and receiving clerks, and passenger booking system operators. The more labour-intensive side of the trade on line crews, Mobile Air Mobility Support teams and loadmaster employment came later in the 1980s. Today, female Traffic Technicians work side-by-side with their male counterparts, whether it be pushing ten thousand pound pallets onto an aircraft or operating ramp and ground-handling vehicles of every shape and description. The author notes that this is a line of work that frequents harsh and hostile environments, and women have been a key part of the team under such conditions for well over a decade. The first female Chief Warrant Officer in the trade, Chief Warrant Officer Gilda Dolph was promoted to that rank in 2006.

In chapter 7, Lieutenant-Commander (retired) Karen Davis shares some of her early experience as a junior leader in the *all female* oceanographic operator trade in the late 1970s and early 1980s, followed by an overview of the socio-legal milestones and CF activities that led to the current status of women in the CF, including the combat arms. She reminds us that women in military leadership positions is certainly not a recent development, but that the establishment of an integrated presence across historically all male domains such as the combat arms does require persistence, ability, and exceptional leadership qualities among those women who are leading the way. This chapter also reinforces the importance of leveraging the experiences of women to gain a full understanding of the challenges of the changing security environment.

Building on research that was conducted in 2003, in chapter 8, Dr. Angela Febbraro offers an analysis of the experiences of several women as well as men in leadership positions in the combat arms. She notes that although women are beginning to be appointed to senior operational leadership positions in the CF, women have not progressed in large numbers to the most senior ranks, particularly in the combat arms. Citing numerous explanations, such as gender stereotyping, in regard to the slow progress of women into leadership roles, Febbraro concludes that women and men in the combat arms value both masculine and feminine leadership characteristics; however, many participants also believe that there are negative implications when female leaders adopt feminine styles of leadership or exhibit feminine characteristics.

In chapter 9, Lieutenant-Commander Lynn Bradley explores the academic literature on leadership styles, with a specific focus on many of the leadership issues raised by the experience of women in the combat arms. Overall, Lieutenant-Commander Bradley suggests that women should neither lead like a man nor adopt women's ways of leading but should capitalize on the wealth of research and information on effective ways of leading men and women. While perhaps reminiscent of situational approaches to leadership, with the diverse workforces of today and the numerous forms of organizations and workgroups, it seems to make the most sense to lead in whatever manner is most effective for the team and the tasks at hand. The author concludes with the observation that research on effectiveness with respect to gender issues in leadership, in particular, appears somewhat sparse and should be extended to include a variety of organizations, industries, and situational contexts as well as extending to more diverse group compositions.

Chapter 10, authored by Dr. Irina Goldenberg and Lieutenant-Commander Gordon AuCoin shed some light on a much-debated topic among military officers – the *pink list* that merit lists and identifies female candidates for attendance on the CF Command and Staff Course for new Lieutenant-Colonels/Commanders and senior Majors/Lieutenant-Commanders. Selection for the Command and Staff Course is an important precursor to further career development and promotion for most officer occupations in the CF and thus represents a competitive process among peers. As operational experience was an important criteria for selection, the list was established as a three-year temporary measure in 1997 to allow those female officers who joined the CF prior to 1989[5] when all occupations and roles were opened for women, and who demonstrated career development potential, to be selected for the course. The authors conclude, based on analysis of selection and attendance rates for the course, that special measures are still required to ensure that women in the CF are accorded equitable opportunity for leadership development.

Although experiences vary and many questions in regard to women and leadership remain unanswered, the contributors to this volume are each successful in conveying important messages about leadership and development as a military *and* female leader. Often, the women profiled in this volume found that it was up to them to develop their own strategies for success. Indeed, every leader has individual responsibilities and will, at times, have to rely on their own ability and resources for solutions to unique circumstances. In addition to the myriad of demands of military service, women have often been unique simply in terms of being women, thus increasing the challenges that have to be overcome. Without question, their experiences will expand the range of strategies available to others who are developing their leadership acumen.

Endnotes

1   See, for example, the discussion presented in Karen D. Davis and Brian McKee, "Women in the Military: Facing the Warrior Framework" in *Challenge and Change in the Military: Gender and Diversity Issues*. Edited by Franklin C. Pinch, Allister T. MacIntyre, Phyllis Browne, and Alan C. Okros. (Kingston, ON: Canadian Defence Academy Press, 2004/2nd printing 2006), 52-75).

2   Barbara Kay, *National Post*. (November 9, 2005), A22.

3   National Defence, *Leadership in the Canadian Forces: Doctrine*. (Canadian Defence Academy – Canadian Forces Leadership Institute, 2005), 3.

4   National Defence, *Leadership in the Canadian Forces: Conceptual Foundations*. (Canadian Defence Academy – Canadian Forces Leadership Institute, 2005), 30.

5   As a result of the 1989 Canadian Human Rights Tribunal ruling all Canadian Forces occupations and roles were opened for female participation.

CHAPTER 1

Gender Integration –
An Asymmetric Environment

Major Anne Reiffenstein

What is success in gender integration? How will we know when we get there? In May 2006, the first female Canadian Forces (CF) officer, Captain Nichola Goddard, died in combat. Her words to me in 2005, on being a woman in the military, provide an important message to all leaders in the CF:

> *Most of all, I want to thank you for showing me that there is nothing to regret or compromise about being a female and being a combat arms officer. You have allowed me to develop my leadership abilities while still being proud of my gender. You have caused me to view being a woman as an asset – not a detriment to my team or to my profession. I can only hope to inspire other women to persevere and take pride in their accomplishments as much as you have for me.*[1]

When all women in the military can say something like this – then I think we are *there!*

Gender integration has met with different measures of success across the different environments in the CF, thus raising the question of whether policies promoting gender integration should be applied universally. As a result of personnel shortages and a dearth of acceptable applicants it is important that the CF attract, and recruit from, any and all possible segments of society, including women. Gender integration, therefore, is essential to the success of the CF. However, gender integration has been more successful in some areas than others, pointing to the need to share and adopt best practices in the less successful areas. Finally, social activism and legislation in Canada have been the primary contributors to gender integration, but it is imperative that CF leadership take the lead in developing and implementing effective policies and practices across the CF.

I have thought long and hard about being able to provide some information that would be relevant to leadership, something constructive that could actually be presented, debated, and put into action. I was at the first Canadian Forces Leadership Institute *Women Leading in Defence* symposium in 2005 when Colonel Cheryl Lamerson, a former staff officer responsible for employment equity and gender integration in the CF, asked "Are we there yet?" That is, has gender integration in the CF been achieved, and to that end, how as an institution will we know when we have achieved integration? What is the magic benchmark? Recently, I also listened to the Chief of the Defence Staff give a speech at a *Women in Defence and Security* luncheon, where he indicated that gender is no longer an issue – merit is how you will be evaluated. Considering these statements, it is clear that there are varying perceptions and measures applied to what has been achieved. If we are accepting that the CF as an institution has achieved what it set out to do with gender integration perhaps then it is time to revisit policies based on gender and its integration.

When I consider gender integration, it is from the perspective of an artillery officer who has spent 10 years in Shilo, Manitoba. I arrived there in 1991, right after a very successful experience in artillery phase training, optimistic and ready to commit to my career as a CF combat arms officer. All I had to do was demonstrate that I was competent, and I would be accepted. Gender would not be an issue. I had already led the gender revolution by completing my phase training. I was Joan of Arc. I was doing it all. Gender integration had been achieved. However, there was some resistance to my presence as an artillery officer. I was fortunate to have a boss who made it clear that gender would not be an issue in his unit, but for the most part I was on my own. The challenges were manageable; however it became clear to me that placing one or two women in a unit does not make gender integration successful. Also, it became more and more clear to me that gender integration was a leadership issue. It was not about male or female. It was about accepting soldiers for who and what they are. Today, I believe that as leaders, we have to come to terms with how leading women is different. Are there differences? We need to identify the correct differences, not the perceived differences, address what is real and get on with it. I think we are still in the process of doing that in the CF.

I have spent most of my career in Shilo, Manitoba. Shilo is an absolutely great training area and the best place in Canada to be a soldier, except in garrison. Everyone, male or female, feels the same way in that regard. The base is 35 kilometers from the nearest town so most of a soldier's social life revolves around the mess. I was the only female in the regiment and the only female officer on the base. The only other women that I had contact with were the spouses of the male officers. These women were quite uncomfortable with me, not because they thought I was after their husbands or that I knew things about their husbands that they did not, but because they did not know how to treat me. I just did not fit in – there was no comfortable slot to put me in. That sense of isolation was with me for some time as a junior officer. I never found a perfect solution, but I had to deal with it. I had a friend who was in a similar situation in the 5e Régiment in Valcartier. We kept in touch by telephone and helped each other through it. There was no active network. No mentorship. There was no one else like me, but it was important to find at least one person with whom I could share my experiences.

I am a product of the regimental system, I am very proud of the regimental system, and I believe in the regimental system. Regardless, the culture of the regimental system has been one of my greatest stumbling blocks. The regimental system has developed through years and years of tradition of exclusive male membership. As leaders, we recognize that it is important to maintain and retain that tradition, but not all of it. It took me about 18 months to realize that there was nothing that I could do to change the attitudes of those who did not think a woman should be in the regiment or did not know what to do with me. The freedom that that realization allowed me was astonishing! I could be myself. I could develop my own leadership style. I could actually do what I thought an artillery officer should do. From that point on, things went really well. I loved what I was doing and enjoyed it immensely.

Of course, I was also the token woman in the regiment. The down side of that is that you become obligated to do some of the tasks even though you feel rather strongly that you do not want to do them. For example, in one instance a brigade commander wanted to have diverse representation on a recruiting poster for the army. I was identified to be the woman on the poster, and even though I made it clear that I did not want to be on the poster, I was not given a choice. Admittedly, being the token woman did afford me some opportunities. Regardless, I was frequently singled out for the wrong reasons. I wanted to perform well and I wanted to be singled out because I was good at what I did, not because I was a woman or the only woman.

From my perspective, the challenge to gender integration today is operating in a gender asymmetric environment. When I say asymmetric environment I am not referring to the three block war, 3D [defence, diplomacy, and development] operations and other characteristics of the changing security environment. I am actually referring to units that have no intention of buying into a diverse army, and in particular in terms of gender – those units that do not have a woman in the place. You walk in and it is exactly the same as the place I walked into as a young officer in the early 1990s – the same people and the same attitudes. No women's washroom except in the medical/health area, and since all the medics have been taken out of the unit, the doors to the women's washroom are locked. You end up there for an entire day of planning and there is not a woman's washroom in the place. The only person you can ask is the Commanding Officer's secretary because she is the only other woman that you can find.

So are we there yet? In my opinion, I should not have to hunt down a woman's washroom, and I should not be the only decision-maker in the room that is not, well…a white guy. We will be there when the command structure, including the most senior non-commissioned members, is as diverse as the junior non-commissioned member corps. In 2004, I was at a command symposium to talk about army transformation and change. We were talking about *change*, and there were only two women in a group of 100 participants. After I graduated from artillery phase training, it was eleven years before another female artillery officer arrived in the unit. That is a long time. That is not evolution, let alone revolution. And that woman experienced many of the same obstacles that I had experienced. In eleven years, the only thing that had changed is that she did not arrive at an all-male regiment – there was one female officer who had arrived eleven years before her.

But we have been working on gender integration in the army. We have resolved many of the training issues, and we have put many programs in place to address recruiting issues. What about army culture? One of the most important things about being a soldier in a combat arms unit is warrior spirit. In my experience, the warrior spirit is a visceral response to adrenaline, aggression, fear, your pride in your unit, and your confidence in your capability. That to me is warrior spirit. It allows you to close and destroy the enemy. It provides you with the motivation to inflict tremendous casualties if necessary, using direct and indirect fire. That is my job – that is what artillery officers do. I plan the delivery of fire support on the ground. In order to do that, you have to inculcate that warrior spirit into your soldiers. You have to make them willing to give up their lives in the service of their country.

The warrior spirit is promoted within an essentially masculine framework. Strength = male; weakness = female. I had a battalion sergeant-major who told the guys who were falling out on a march, 'You are marching like a bunch of women'. I pointed out to him that he said, 'women' as if it was a bad thing. In the training system, we have told the instructors that they can no longer promote masculine expressions that imply that feminine is weak, but we have not told them what to say instead. We have not developed an inclusive strategy for promoting and developing the warrior spirit. In fact, I have adopted the warrior spirit and I have caught myself saying 'Don't be such a woman'! I believe that leadership needs to support further understanding of the warrior spirit, so that it can be developed in a way that does not denigrate gender or any other social perspective.

So that leaves me with many questions in terms of what defines success in gender integration? Is it qualitative and quantitative? What should the benchmark be? If there is a benchmark or target, why are there still leaders who do not know about it? If there is no magic number, that implies a qualitative focus. Indeed, that reinforces the argument that the CF is looking for the best person for the job, regardless of gender. Is the mere presence of women in every avenue of service within the CF is enough? Should a qualitative assessment of women's experience be required? Should retention be used as the measure for success? Should the number of senior officers in key decision-making positions be used as a measure? Is the lack of negative media exposure on gender issues a solid indicator; that is, is no news good news? I do not believe that we can declare success or be confident that policies are working without defining where the organization should be.

Women serving in the military have varying opinions and perspectives about gender integration policies. Are they required? Should you participate? Are the policies that ushered in gender integration still relevant? There seems to be great variance in applications of gender integration policy – is that an indicator of irrelevance or ignorance? The many policies and programs that were used to usher in gender integration, have had mixed reviews. The Standard for Harassment and Racism Prevention (SHARP) and diversity awareness training were reviled as exercises in political correctness – they were not terribly constructive. Universally loathed by almost all personnel, they were perceived to be invariably the result of some embarrassing stories about the CF that appeared in the media. Are these programs still required? Is the lack of embarrassing stories appearing in the media an indicator of success? From my perspective, professional development related to diversity and gender integration has fallen by the wayside due to the operational tempo of the CF. Perhaps gender integration is so far down the road that we need to take a look at program relevance and determine whether we need to continue with a daughter of SHARP. Or perhaps we need to identify the road ahead depending on what we view as success.

The critical mass policy has resulted in asymmetric gender integration and has resulted in organizations that have no female officer, senior non-commissioned officers (NCOs) or soldiers, at least in the army environment. There are infantry battalions that have never had a female officer wear their cap badge. When I raised this observation with a senior officer, I was told that it was not important and there was no requirement to have female officers, as soldiers were soldiers. In another instance, a senior officer said that there is no indication that anyone will try to change that situation in a direct manner.

Whenever I hear statements that imply or confirm that gender integration has been achieved, I think of my very recent conversation with a very fit, intelligent Officer Cadet (OCdt) who wants to be an infantry officer but does not want the stigma of being the first female officer in the regiment. Her perception is that in spite of successful completion of four years of military college, her gender will work to her detriment if she chooses that career path within the military. There is no effective 'critical mass' in the combat arms, nor is there a strategy in place to counter the impacts of social and professional isolation. Many subtle and underlying cultural influences have not been seriously addressed from a gender perspective. 'It is a leadership issue' is the only strategy to ensure that 'minority' members of the CF become integrated into the larger whole.

Contrast the junior infantry officer with a lieutenant-colonel communications and electronics engineering (CELE) officer who is the commanding officer of an air force unit. She leads a unit that has equal numbers of men and women at all rank levels. In this case, gender integration is not even on the table as an issue. Gender integration has been achieved, there are few or no organizational difficulties, and the gender integration programs are at best irrelevant to the operations of her organization. Most of the air force officers I have spoken with, and in particular those in the support trades, no longer see this as any sort of relevant issue, and thus do not support any of the gender integration policies in place.

One particular policy, commonly dubbed the *pink list*,[2] has been universally condemned by officers who are in tight competition for positions at the CF Command and Staff Course (CSC) as unfair and allowing women to have an unfair advantage over their male counterparts. Female colleagues have indicated to me that they would be unwilling to go to the CF CSC in a *pink seat* as it would undermine their credibility and have refused it when offered. A senior officer once told me with considerable pride, that one of his female subordinates refused to accept the *pink seat* that she had not earned the same way as her peers and that in fact any competent female officer would make the same choice. Many female officers believe that use of the pink list is of greater detriment than assistance to gender integration. In fact, many of them also believe that the program should be cancelled as it has outlasted its relevancy. One of the difficulties is that few people know how the *pink list* works which results in a number of different attitudes. It is a policy that needs to be re-evaluated periodically for relevancy and to determine whether it is continuing to achieve the intended aim, whatever that may be.

Finally, there are many who say that the policies are irrelevant as gender integration can only be achieved through time. Evolution vice revolution – evolution of a military culture cannot be achieved overnight but the transformation is well on its way. Gender integration will not be achieved through special programs but will be achieved through the passage of time. Discussions amongst some serving women highlight once again the asymmetry of gender integration in the CF. Those organizations where there is significant female presence at all rank levels and positions believe that things have evolved quite quickly, while others in units that have little female representation view gender integration as a long-term and risky evolutionary process.

So what conclusions can you draw from this discussion? Do we still require the existing policies with respect to gender integration? I think an important question to consider in arriving at the estimate is, 'Has the situation changed?' The answer to this is 'yes'. The situation has changed and we need to respond with policies that acknowledge that change, and are applied only where necessary. Perhaps instead of looking at gender integration from an umbrella point of view, it needs to be more tailored to areas that are having difficulty with gender integration. For example, a CELE officer in Development Phase (DP) 2 would require no gender integration policy, while a colleague in infantry DP 2 requires the support of a gender integration policy that applies to selection for critical career courses until a certain number of female infantry officers have successfully completed that particular phase (DP 2 in this case). This is a model very loosely based on the Welsh Parliamentary system of government that initially mandated an identified number of women who must be in the legislature, followed by gradual removal of the requirements as more women were selected to run for elected office. The intent was to ensure that there was appropriate representation of women in government, employing an evolution strategy to move from mandated participation to elected participation. This policy was extremely effective as the Welsh have very strong female representation in their government.

Finally, it is important to collect the patchwork of policies, ensure that they are comprehensive and relevant, and make leadership accountable for implementation. Commanding Officers should be required to indicate why they have no female officers, no female NCOs, and/or no soldiers in their units. The unit should be red flagged as a unit that requires particular attention for policy application. Integration needs to be at a universal level in order to achieve an inclusive end state.

Going back full circle to Colonel Lamerson's question on gender integration in the CF – how will we know when we get *there?* We will know we are there when women in the combat arms: have no regrets about becoming a soldier; have the full support of their superiors, peers, and subordinates to fully develop their leadership abilities; feel pride in being a woman, a soldier, and an asset to their team and their profession; and take pride in inspiring both women and men to follow in their footsteps.

Endnotes

1   Captain Nichola Kathleen Sarah Goddard, to author, 20 June 2005. Captain Goddard, an artillery officer with 1 Royal Canadian Horse Artiller, was killed in a battle with Taliban forces in Afghanistan 17 May 2006. She was the first Canadian female combat arms soldier to die while engaged on a combat mission.

2   A female list is created, in addition to the primary and alternate candidate lists, in order to fill up to five additional seats with the five most deserving female candidates that would not otherwise be selected. The selection board derives this additional *female* list by ranking the top female candidates who meet the basic Staff College student profile and who are not on the primary lists. Dr. Irina Goldenberg and Lieutenant-

Commander Gordon AuCoin, "Special Selection Program for Female Selection to Canadian Forces Command and Staff Course" in this volume. Originally published by Defence Research and Development Canada, Centre for Operational Research and Analysis, Technical Memorandum 2006-11, April 2006.

CHAPTER 2

Embracing Challenge and Opportunity: 30 Years of Progress

Commodore Margaret F. Kavanagh

After 30 years as an officer and a woman in the Canadian Forces (CF) I can honestly say "we have come a long way baby". I believe it is important that our young female officers understand the opportunities that they enjoy, and they should cherish and respect them, because these opportunities have not always been available. Indeed my initial attempts to join the CF were actually thwarted because as a physical education major at university, I was not allowed to become a physical education officer due to the fact that this occupation was only open to men in the early 1970s. Fortunately for me, and I hope the CF, I decided to pursue a career in medicine so my career took a completely different path. Over the ensuing paragraphs I will relate some of my personal experiences and conclude with my lessons learned about life in the military as a woman, commitment to something that you believe in, and leadership.

I once related my story to a group of young female lieutenants at a mess dinner and the look on their faces was one of disbelief! However, I can assure you that what I am about to relate is indeed the truth. I came to duty as a captain general duty medical officer in the summer of 1979 after completing all of my medical training. At that time women were not allowed to serve at sea, with any of the Army field units, not even in support occupations, or fly aircraft. Consequently, operational tours of duty for women were non-existent. The early 1980s opened up opportunities for women to serve in 'non-traditional' roles with 4 Canadian Mechanized Brigade Group in Germany and aboard Her Majesty's Canadian Ship (HMCS) *Cormorant*. Despite several attempts to go to Germany, I was advised that the CF had its quota of women and I was not allowed to take on such a position. Subsequently, and purely by chance, I sat beside a senior medical officer at a mess dinner one night. Over the course of the dinner he persuaded me to take a chance with the navy and volunteer for sea duty, hence my naval uniform. Consequently, I became the first female medical officer to serve at sea aboard the only ship open to women at the time, HMCS *Cormorant*. Given that *Cormorant* was a diving ship and my duties included treating diving injuries, I felt it was important to understand the environment in which the divers worked. Even though I was already qualified as a Ship's Diving Medical Officer, I pursued my Ship's Diver qualification. As a result I became one of only a very few women qualified as a Ship's Diver. Regulations at the time allowed only women posted to the *Cormorant* to take diving training and when posted off the ship, the qualification was rescinded. The justification for this was that women would not require this qualification in any other position hence there was no need to retain the qualification. Interestingly, a male army cook who just might be serving a tour at sea was not subject to this same restriction even though he may spend the rest of his career in the field force. I became aware of this regulation when the west coast Navy refused to train me on the first of my two re-qualification courses. Instead I returned to the east coast, a location that I had only left the year previous, and succeeded in obtaining my re-qualification. Three years after the initial refusal to re-qualify, the regulations were changed and I re-qualified a second time at the Pacific diving unit.

During the 1980s, many more opportunities opened up to women in the CF including the Royal Military College, employment in operational units in support occupations and even flying aircraft. It was not until later that all occupations and operational experiences opened up to women. My own operational experience began with my assignment as the senior medical advisor (J1 Med) at the CF headquarters in Bahrain during the Persian Gulf Conflict in 1991. I was the only female senior officer on the Commander's staff. With no previous operational experience I was thrust into a position for which I was less than fully prepared. Having said that, I made the best of all opportunities to learn and accept advice from my fellow officers. This twist of fate tweaked my interest and precipitated a desire to be more engaged in the operational aspects of the CF. To that end I volunteered to take on the role as Commanding Officer of 1 Canadian Field Hospital, which at that time was only an augmentee position that was activated only when the unit exercised or deployed. I had the honour of commanding this unit on two major Army exercises over a three-year period. Subsequently, I also had the honour and privilege of being the first woman to command a Regular Force Field Ambulance when I assumed command of 1 Field Ambulance in Calgary in 1994. During this tenure, I deployed numerous members of my unit to operational tours of duty around the world irrespective of their gender. That, I believe, is the mark of success in terms of gender integration. I personally completed all of the pre-deployment training for a mission within the United Nations Protection Force (UNPROFOR) in the former Yugoslavia but did not deploy because the task was shifted to a NATO mission and given to another CF organization.

After my tour as Commanding Officer, 1 Field Ambulance, I held numerous staff positions in National Defence Headquarters culminating in my current position as Director General Health Services/Commander Canadian Forces Health Services Group. I am the first Regular Force female Commodore. This sent shock waves through the supply system when we attempted to sort out the unique components of my uniform. The last and only female Commodore retired from the Reserve Force in the mid 1990s.

The aforementioned history lesson is not meant to highlight my accomplishments, but rather to outline some of the systemic challenges that women have faced in pursuing a career in the CF. Why bother you might ask, a question that is at the crux of the issue. I believe that for women, like their male colleagues, a career in the CF is not just a job. It is indeed a vocation and a way of life. You have to truly believe that what you are doing is for a greater cause (i.e. service to the country before yourself) to continually face up to these challenges. I know that as a female officer I have as much to offer as my male counterparts and if I have to prove it through my actions, I will.

There are some specific teaching points inherent in my experiences that I would like to share. The opportunity to serve at sea was indeed a twist of fate. These opportunities and challenges should be taken up when they occur because one never knows how it will turn out. Interesting challenges are a component of life in the CF and they help us grow and develop as people and as leaders. If there are roadblocks being put in one's way that prevent achievement of a specific goal, do not give up. Do not be afraid to take on the challenge of fighting for what you believe is right and just. Take up a challenge and pursue your dream.

Credibility and trustworthiness with individuals in the organization are fundamental to one's success. Take up the challenges and gain experiences to be as credible as the male members of the CF. By the same token, one cannot expect any favouritism or privilege based upon gender. If the job needs doing, it needs to be done irrespective of gender. This is not to say that we can be all things to all people and that we have to know everything. Rather it is important to understand your shortfalls in training, experience or personal attributes, and find ways to minimize or mitigate these shortcomings.

The old saying, 'you have to be twice as good to get half the credit' has applied to female members of the CF in the past; however, I believe that for the most part it no longer exists. There are still obstacles, albeit much smaller ones, being placed before us because women at the most senior ranks are still a relatively novel concept. However, it is recognition that integrity, commitment and a fundamental belief in 'Duty with Honour' are at the core of why anyone belongs to the CF, regardless of gender, that will ultimately make women successful within the CF. As leaders we must 'walk the talk' by behaving in ways that demonstrate the values of the CF and be committed to the organization and its mission.

CHAPTER 3

Building Trust and Credibility
at Home and Abroad

Major (retired) Sue Forgues

When I was first approached to contribute a paper concerning women in leadership roles in the Canadian Forces (CF), I was not sure whether I would be able to craft such a document. Suggestions for the paper included experiences with cross-cultural values, resistance to women in leadership roles, barriers to effective leadership and dealing with ethical dilemmas. Truthfully, I had given little 'organized' thought to any of the above issues and, frankly, I was not sure I wanted to re-examine my career as a tactical helicopter (tac hel) pilot from this perspective. However, the more I reflected on my 16 years in the CF, the more I realized that I had been a part of a unique transition within the CF – the introduction of women into combat roles. I also began to realize that I had encountered nearly all of the aforementioned experiences at one time or another throughout my career. After digging through my boxes of paraphernalia in the basement, perusing countless photo albums and journals, and re-tracing my flying career in my logbook, I was ready to commit to paper my perspectives and experiences as a woman in an operational leadership role

PART 1: General Leadership

Leadership Theory

As the distinguished Sun Tzu once said:

> Leadership is a matter of intelligence, trustworthiness, humaneness, courage and sternness. Every general has heard of these five things. Those who know them prevail, those who do not know them do not prevail.[1]

In the early years of my career, I candidly admit that formal leadership theory held little interest for me since pilot training occupied nearly all of my time. However, upon reflection, even as a student, I was influenced by those in leadership roles – primarily my instructors. After I had achieved my wings and was posted to my first operational squadron, my time remained occupied with taskings, proficiency checks and other flying related duties. Even during this very busy time, my own leadership style continued to be moulded through observation and experience, as those around me in leadership roles once continued to have an active influence on my behaviour.

Duty with Honour: The Profession of Arms in Canada defines leadership as the use of authority and influence to accomplish the defence mission in a professional manner.[2] The key word in that definition is 'professional'; I believe that professional competency is the cornerstone of military leadership. As a pilot, I spent my entire career improving my professional competency and I have no reason to believe it is any different in any other military occupation. To be professionally incompetent is to intentionally put lives at risk. Besides, who is going to follow someone who does not really know what they are doing? Professional competency for pilots is a rigorous process comprising both demonstrable skills and academic knowledge; aircraft/flying limitations, rules of the air, operational restrictions, technical proficiency, category rides, instrument exams – the list is seemingly endless. Those pilots who inspire others to follow them are those who know both their aircraft and themselves inside and out. It is the pilots who do not break rules, who do not exceed limitations, and who remember that they are part of a crew, who become leaders. As I gained experience, I gravitated towards those I admired and watched them closely, in an effort to emulate them. This 'informal' leadership experience instilled in me qualities that I strived to maintain the rest of my career.

The pilots who influenced me most were those who quietly did their job – no bravado, no grandstanding, no bragging; they simply strapped in and flew the aircraft. Their quiet strength and confidence in their own abilities made me realize that the only person I had anything to prove to was myself. I wanted to be the best pilot I could be because I simply would not settle for anything less. As a woman, this leadership style had (and still has) immense appeal. Throughout my career, I found myself under the proverbial 'microscope' and, each time I relied on my belief in my own professional competency and just got on with the job at hand.

However, it did not take long for me to realize that professional competency alone does not make a military leader. Everyone who reads this chapter will know someone who is great at their job but fails to inspire others to accomplish the mission. The missing ingredient in their leadership style is communication – they fail to motivate, solve problems, make decisions, mentor, or foster teamwork. When I conjure up the names of those who most influenced my career, they were, without exception, excellent communicators. Persuasive and facilitative leaders, they recognized and encouraged leadership potential in their subordinates.

I am certain that my interpretation of effective leadership and how I applied it in my own career differs significantly from my male counterparts. When I enrolled in the CF in 1988, there were few women pilots and no women tac hel pilots. Like all student pilots, I had a very steep learning curve and I had to work very hard to build my professional competency. It was during my time in Moose Jaw that I encountered what I came to call the "100/0 factors". It is second nature to automatically assess the personality, skills and competency of those we associate with professionally. That assessment generally takes two forms:

1. We assume that the individual we have encountered is professionally competent until they prove otherwise (the '100' factor) or,

2. We assume that the individual we have encountered is professionally incompetent until they can prove otherwise (the '0' factor).

Undoubtedly, for a significant portion of my career, I was considered part of the '0' factor. Either through actions or words, I was left with no doubt that until there was proof to the contrary, I simply did not belong in the cockpit. In hindsight, I can say that I am glad that I had faith in my own abilities since there were lots of folks who did not. In many ways, I am thankful for their skepticism as it helped me become a better pilot and to value those whose belief in my professional competency ensured my continued professional growth.

Military Culture

> As a result of its distinctive mandate and the need to instill organizational loyalty and obedience, most military organizations develop a culture unto themselves, distinguished by an emphasis on hierarchy, tradition, rituals and customs, and distinctive dress and insignias.[3]

The culture of the CF changed significantly during the 16-year period in which I served. I was enrolled as a pilot in the CF in 1988. Only three years earlier, the classification had been opened to new women recruits, even though it had opened for women already serving in the CF in 1980. The announcement was made in 1989, just after I started pilot training in Moose Jaw, that women would be allowed in combat roles – including tactical helicopters. The following year, when I received my wings in Portage La Prairie, I had the distinction of being the first woman tac hel pilot to be posted to 408 Squadron (Sqn) in Edmonton. My male counterparts at 408 were probably as unsure about how I would fit in there as I was. Given the enormous amount of time spent in the field, my presence raised all kinds of questions about sleeping arrangements, socializing and acceptable behaviour. On our initial field deployment, serious consideration was given to having me bunk in with the squadron supply officer (who was a woman). With all the courage I could muster, I nixed the idea and 'demanded' to reside with my male counterparts, all of who were in the same tent. An ingenious arrangement of tent liners resulted in my being able to 'live' with the guys and I tried very hard throughout my career not to be 'segregated' unless it was operationally imperative. Women now routinely deploy domestically and internationally with their male counterparts and I hope that, in some small way, I may have contributed to the acceptance of their presence in the field.

My presence at 408 Sqn did not escape the attention of the wives of my fellow pilots and, initially, there was open hostility from some of them. In many cases, I deployed on tasking with their husbands for days (even weeks) at a time; they didn't know me and, therefore, they feared the unknown. I made a concerted effort to get to know these women and to have them understand that the squadron was my place of work and not a social club. Using the '100/0 factors' once again, I asked that these women trust me until I proved myself untrustworthy. To their credit, the majority of them did and I am still friends with several of these women to this day.

Personal Leadership Strategies

> To be persuasive, we must be believable; to be believable, we must be credible; to be credible we must be truthful.[4]

This particular section of the chapter compelled me to take a hard look at my own leadership style and effectiveness and to assess the strategies that worked for me. Using *Duty with Honour* as a guide, I have assessed my own leadership style as ranging between persuasive and supportive.[5] As you can surmise, this is a pretty broad range and very much situation-dependent. As I discussed earlier, much of my own leadership style resulted from observing my colleagues. I remained cognizant of the fact that the leadership style that may work for one person may not work for another until it has been tailored to that individual's personality and style.

I have always been an extrovert and this aspect of my personality pervades every part of my life, most certainly my leadership style. I have always welcomed the opportunity to improve myself, "to learn from experience and from those who have experience".[6] Having given it considerable thought, I have drafted what I feel are the five key components of my personal leadership strategy:

1. Be professionally credible through ongoing professional development and education. Know your aircraft's limitations as well as your own and use extreme caution when exceeding either.

2. Communicate effectively. Communication isn't just about giving a really slick presentation or writing an excellent briefing note. It's about ensuring that what you say is understood. Communicating is also about listening – not just hearing.

3. Demonstrate integrity in everything you do. Nothing can destroy confidence in your leadership abilities faster than a perceived loss of integrity. Trust is earned and, once lost, it is difficult to regain.

4. Treat subordinates fairly. Having spent my entire flying career as part of a crew and squadron, I realized that each member of my crew had a specific professional capability. I listened to them and learned from them. As a flight commander, I made time to visit with the sections of my flight and get to know each person.

5. Focus on the team and the mission. No one works alone, not even pilots. To get the plane in the air, ground crew, administrative staff, operations personnel and aircrew all have to come together as a team. To forget that is to do an incredible disservice to those we work with. Never forget the mission – as *Duty with Honour* points out: mission success is about the primacy of operations – accomplish the mission.[7]

Per Ardua Ad Astra (Through Adversity to the Stars)

The Air Force motto recognizes that there will be times of adversity, when, no matter how much effort you put into an activity, how thoroughly you have briefed the mission, how carefully you have crafted your briefing, something will go wrong. The *Canadian Oxford Dictionary* defines adversity as "the condition of adverse fortune".[8] Adversity can range in scale from these aforementioned challenges through to the death of someone under your command. While my leadership experience in dealing with adversity is decidedly limited, when I did face it, I focused on what I needed to do to cope with it; a plan of action so-to-speak. When adversity affected my colleagues or subordinates, I offered my support and friendship.

Certainly, each of us responds to adversity and the stress it produces in our own fashion. Dealing with stress for me was relatively straightforward: rather than dwelling on the past, I focused on the mission and formulated a plan of action.

There is no doubt that the first two years of my military career as a student pilot were the most stressful of my life. Failure on any part of flying training would have made me permanently unsuitable for employment as a pilot in the CF – now that's pressure!! Basic Flying Training (BFT) in Portage La Prairie did not go as smoothly as I would have liked and I found myself on a 'do-or-die' ride for my final flight test. As I did so often later in my career, I relied on my professional competency – I knew how to fly that aircraft, I just had to make sure the testing officer knew it. I studied and rehearsed every aspect of that flight in my head and on the day of the flight test, I aced the trip. In Moose Jaw, at the 'Big 2",[9] the pressure mounted. Having failed my first flight test, I knew that I could not fail any of the next five. If I had, I would probably have been taken off the course. The quest for professional competency spurred me on throughout Moose Jaw, and again in Portage la Prairie at Basic Helicopter School. For over a year, I studied incessantly, went to bed early every night, and practiced my checks in the simulators. I ate, slept, lived and breathed flying and, in the end, was awarded my wings in October 1990. This became a familiar pattern throughout my career – study, practice, learn! I also relied on my personal support system – my mother, my brother, my good friends and fellow pilots. Each added their own perspective to the challenge I faced and I used their energies to refocus my own. All of them deserve to share in my successes; any failures however, are my own doing!

PART II: Operational Leadership Roles

During my career, I was fortunate to deploy three times: Somalia in 1993 when I was with 408 Sqn, Bosnia in 1995 as part of the British Rapid Reaction Force, and Zaire in 1997 as a member of a Royal Air Force (RAF) Puma contingent.

Somalia — 1993

In January 1993, I deployed overseas for the first time. Briefly, the Canadian Airborne Regiment (Cdn AB Regt) had been sent to Somalia (Belet Huen to be exact) as part of a Canadian peacekeeping force. The Airborne was receiving their helicopter support from the Sea King detachment aboard HMCS *Preserver*, anchored off of Mogadishu. The Sea King was a venerable workhorse for anti-submarine warfare but the crews had little training in working with the army, which of course was (and remains to this day) the 'bread and butter' of tac hel, which was flying Twin Hueys at the time.

The Airborne had a demonstrable need for helicopter support for its reconnaissance, resupply and convoys but were experiencing difficulty in communicating those needs to the Sea King detachment. 427 Sqn in Petawawa was gearing up for full-scale deployment to the theatre so the decision was made to send two tac hel pilots from 408 Sqn as "translators" until 427 arrived.

After an arduous two-day trip, a colleague and I arrived in theatre and were assaulted by the heat and smell of 'Mog' (the in-theatre name for Mogadishu). Initially, we stayed onboard HMCS *Preserver*, which proved an interesting experience for me personally. There were no women Sea King pilots on the detachment and, given the restricted space available onboard, I was billeted with the doctor. As I discussed earlier, I really hated being separated from the rest of the aircrew but you have to pick your battles carefully and, given the space constraints aboard the ship, I realized that I would never win this one. Instead, I asked one of the Sea King pilots to ensure I was included in their briefings and, thanks to his efforts, I never missed out.

This deployment differed from my future deployments insofar as I had no subordinates in theatre. However, I did work very closely with members of the Cdn AB Regt who regarded me with thinly veiled contempt initially. In 1993, there were few women pilots in tac hel and collectively we had a minimal deployment history. In order to become more familiar with their mission, I volunteered to be a co-driver in a road move from Mogadishu to

Belet Huen. The Airborne would provide a secure escort for the food trucks and non-governmental organizations in the convoy. The result: ten hours in a closed truck on the worst highway I have ever seen with an Ethiopian truck driver who spoke no English. However, when we got to Belet Huen, the Airborne made space for me in their visitor's tent where I bunked for two nights while I conducted reconnaissance (recce'd) of the 427 Sqn site next door to them. I made an effort to meet as many of the soldiers as possible and kept my mouth shut about the rather sparse accommodations. It was the highlight of my deployment!

It was a new experience to be armed with live ammunition and I wore a 9 mm pistol the entire time in theatre. Thankfully, I never had to use my weapon but it was unsettling driving through a foreign city with a round chambered in my 9 mm. I placed my trust in the driver who negotiated some of the narrowest streets I had ever seen, and the Army escorts who traveled with wooden clubs to discourage anyone reaching into the vehicle to steal.

On our return to Canada a month later, we were tasked to debrief a cadre of senior officers on our experiences in theatre. This was a first for me and I felt a little overwhelmed being, not only a 'mere' Captain but also the only woman in the room. I punctuated the debrief with anecdotes and observations about the Somali culture and its people and I passed around some photos I had taken. The debrief was well received and I was subsequently tasked to write both newspaper and magazine articles[10] about my experiences. The lesson I took away from my first deployment was this: Pay attention to the land and the people into which you are deployed. Listen to those who are deployed with you and learn from their experiences. The lesson stood me in good stead on my next deployment two years later.

Royal Air Force Exchange – 1994

In January 1994, my flight commander at 408 Sqn approached me concerning an exchange position as a Puma pilot in Odiham, United Kingdom (UK). I had two questions: Where's Odiham and what's a Puma? After a little research, I put my name forward as a candidate only to have it rejected given that the Royal Air Force (RAF) did not have any women Puma pilots of its own. To say I reacted badly to the news would be something of an understatement. Throughout my career, and in life in general, I had never decided on a course of action or accepted a challenge because I wanted to wave the "I am a woman and I can do this" flag. Instead, I had based my actions and choices on the belief that I should be entitled to do something in accordance with my abilities; my request for the exchange position was no different. I had flown Twin Hueys for three and a half years, I was an aircraft Captain, a scheduling officer, a maintenance test pilot and was mountain flying qualified. I was also slated to attend the Advanced Aviation Course (for tac hel pilots, the most advanced tactics course we did at the time) and was approaching eligibility for promotion to Major. In the end, I was granted the exchange, not because my qualifications overawed the RAF but rather, because they had course loaded their own woman Puma pilot onto the next Puma course and they would now accept me on the exchange. I landed in the UK on the 50th Anniversary of D-Day – 06 June 1994 – and joined 33 Sqn RAF. My four years with them would change how I viewed myself as both a pilot and an officer.

Bosnia – 1995

Role:

- the Rapid Reaction Force (RRF) will <u>enhance</u> UNPROFOR's ability to undertake its mission more effectively by:
    - improving UNPROFOR's ability to protect itself;
    - enabling UNPROFOR to react more quickly;
    - demonstrating our resolve and thus increasing deterrence.
- the RRF will <u>not</u> be used for peace enforcement (<u>for which no mandate exists</u>) and will therefore <u>not transform the strategic situation</u>.[11]

By mid-1995, the situation within Bosnia-Herzegovina had deteriorated drastically and news around the world reported extensive fighting around Mostar and in the Bihac pocket. The North Atlantic Treaty Organization (NATO) had taken an active role in what was happening inside the Former Republic of Yugoslavia and, in August 1995, a British Rapid Reaction Force comprising elements of 24 Airmobile Brigade, was deployed to Croatia to assist UNPROFOR. The contingent was based in Croatia, at Ploce, a dockyard town located on the Adriatic coast halfway between Split and Dubrovnik. The RAF deployed six Puma helicopters and four Chinooks to provide airlift support to 24 Brigade. This, coupled with the Army Air Corps Gazelle and Lynx fleet that had also deployed, resulted in a significant helicopter presence in theatre. The deployment marked a first in my career; although I had deployed previously, this was the first time I had taken a helicopter into a theatre of war. The threat of Surface to Air Missiles (SAMs) and small arms fire was very real and my crew and I had spent a lot of time prior to the deployment rehearsing low-level evasion and nap of the earth flying.

Before we deployed, the decision was made to fly constituted crews in theatre. A Puma crew comprises a pilot, a navigator and a crewman and I was pleased with the two individuals chosen as my crew. Although we had flown together previously, none us of had flown in a theatre of war before and I decided we needed to sit down, as a crew, and talk about the deployment. We divided up the duties: I would be responsible for passing along all theatre intelligence reports and for gathering information on known weapons systems and threat envelopes. Additionally, the Puma had been modified with Infrared (IR) jammers, with which none of us were familiar. Consequently, getting information on how to employ the system effectively was also my responsibility. My navigator (I will call him B) would be responsible for compiling all maps and global positioning system (GPS) information concerning landing zones and airports in theatre. He also helped plan the deployment into theatre – a two-day flight of six Pumas through France and Italy. Our crewman (I will call him D) looked after aircraft configuration, weapons (each of us was issued with a rifle and a 9 mm pistol), and the technical aspects of the IR jammers. Each of us then had a crucial role in preparing for the deployment and these responsibilities carried into theatre as well.

One of the more difficult aspects of the deployment was the advanced planning of our actions should we be forced to land inside hostile territory and have to escape and evade capture. This had already happened previously to an American fighter pilot (Scott O'Grady) and two French fighters were shot down shortly after we arrived in Ploce. While the RAF had provided us with survival kits, portable GPS units, weapons and standard operating procedures (SOPs), I felt we needed to discuss, in detail, our actions once we were on the ground, especially if we had troops on board. The three of us spent hours throughout the deployment refining our plan and, as such, really came together as a crew. We would, of course, rely on our training to the maximum extent possible, but our survival really depended on our working as a team. Interestingly, there were few other crews that adopted the same philosophy. In hindsight, I think I put a lot of emphasis on this planning to ensure that my crew knew that, as a woman and as a Canadian, I was committed to them as their pilot and that I valued their professional input. In total, I flew 27 missions in theatre and, thankfully, we never had to put our escape and evasion plan into action.

We were, however, illuminated by missile radar on a return flight from Split. Briefly, a missile system employs search radar to locate possible targets. Once the target is acquired, the missile can be launched. As we started our approach into Ploce, the radar warning receiver lit up and emitted a high pitched tone. As we had practiced so many times in the UK, B called the direction of the 'spike' while I turned the aircraft away from that direction and D cleared us through the turn. After ensuring we were behind a ridgeline for the remainder of the descent, we landed without further incident. In our crew debrief, we talked about the incident and I realized that none of us had questioned the decisions or commands of the others. We fell back on our training, and each of us performed our crew duties as we had briefed. I have to admit, I was really proud of our crew!

The British engineers had done a remarkable job in preparing Ploce dockyard for our arrival but, in reality, we were camped at sea level on the Adriatic coast, facing an onslaught of autumn storms. The first hit us three weeks into the deployment and a number of tents were blown away, although thankfully none of the RAF aircrew tents went missing. I shared a tent with two British women aircrew – a pilot and a crewman – and, fortunately, our tent remained bone-dry. The same could not be said for some of our male counterparts and, in particular, the Royal Anglian Infantry regiment with whom we shared the dockyard. Several soldiers had broken collarbones and arms thanks to flying steel tent frames and many had lost their kit. After the storm, the camp was flooded and the area contaminated by human waste that had been washed out of the camp toilet facilities. The storm had contaminated our drinking water and food and, even worse, there were two cases of leptospirosis in the camp.[12] We were marginally better prepared for the second storm which hit in mid-September, however, when storm three hit less than a week later, we evacuated Ploce and headed inland for the duration of the deployment.

Zaire – 1997

Attention was once again focused on Africa in early 1997 when Laurent Kabila began a coup against President Mobutu of Zaire. Zaire had been a troubled country for more than a decade and, only four years earlier, had been witness to terrible crimes against Belgian nuns and other civilians caught in a civil uprising near Kinshasa, the capital city.[13] When tensions again flared, the British Foreign and Commonwealth Office tasked a Puma contingent to deploy to Brazzaville in the (then) Congo, across the river from Kinshasa, Zaire to be prepared to extract civilians as part of a non-combatant extraction operation.[14]

On 1 May 1997, four Pumas and a contingent of approximately 70 RAF personnel deployed by C5 Galaxy into theatre. The expectation was that, upon arrival in Libreville in the Gabon, the crews, with minimal rest, would reassemble the Pumas (the main rotor blades had been removed for transport on the C5) and test fly them so that we could forward stage to Brazzaville the next day. The flight time from the UK to the Gabon was approximately 16 hours and to assist personnel in getting crew rest on the flight over, we were all given temazepam.[15] I am usually a very good sleeper, however, on occasion when it has been noisy in the field, or my body clock has been disrupted by night flying, I have not been well rested. Given the enormity of the task that faced us in Libreville, I elected to take the medication and it definitely worked for me. I crawled under the seats onboard the C5 and the next thing I remember was landing in Libreville. Both my navigator and my crewman had also passed out so we all started the deployment similarly 'refreshed'.[16]

The four Pumas arrived in Brazzaville and made camp on the airfield, which we shared with a French Puma detachment and two Belgian helicopters being piloted by Belgian mercenaries (their words). Additionally, a United States (US) Marine Expeditionary Unit with Cobras onboard was anchored just off the Congo coast. We were briefed that several extraction points had been set up inside Kinshasa to facilitate evacuation of civilians, however, little had been done to ensure that only civilians would be transported and even less had been done to ensure the safety of the helicopter crews once the civilians were onboard. We also pointed out that the capture of a British Puma would significantly enhance the capabilities of either side in the conflict, particularly the Zairian Air Force that, at that time, had no helicopters. We were to fly as a constituted crew and, once again, as I had done with crew in Bosnia, I divided up the crew duties and then sat down with my navigator and crewman and talked through the mission. All of us had serious concerns about carrying non-secure passengers so we came up with a contingency plan should any of them brandish a weapon or attempt to hijack our helicopter. Once again, this advance planning solidified our crew.

Living conditions were austere to say the least – a tent on an airfield that was littered with broken-down aircraft and old hangars. There was no running water, only bottled, and meals were the British versions of meals ready to eat (MREs). We soon found out that the French versions had wine in them so we did a bit of 'horsetrading' with the French for some of their rations! There were five crews for four helicopters so we lived one crew to a tent and we shared sanitation facilities with the Gurkhas who were living in the old hangar adjacent to our site. Interestingly, I realized after we arrived in theatre that I was the only woman on the detachment. This posed some interesting challenges for washroom and ablution facilities but, in the end, the arrangement worked like a charm.

Tactically, the National Evacuation Operation (NEO) mission we were assigned was fraught with danger. The extraction points inside Kinshasa were all in the middle of heavily populated areas; one was, in fact, less than a kilometer from the garrison of the Division de la Securité du Président, Mobutu's private Army. Nearly all of the RAF aircrew on the deployment had flown in Northern Ireland and were well versed in getting in and out of landing zones in built up areas. I had not served in Northern Ireland and faced the rather daunting task of learning new helicopter tactics while deployed in theatre. This situation did little to inspire my crew's confidence in my abilities but, to their credit, they were extremely professional and, given that each had served multiple tours in Northern Island, they proved invaluable.

On our second week in theatre, we were placed on ten minutes notice to move when one of the extraction points missed a scheduled check in. For the first time in my career, I was genuinely afraid that I might not return from a mission. I also realized that I was not the only one who was afraid – I was, however, the only one who would openly admit it. So, I sat down with my crew and we talked through the trip, studied the maps, explored contingencies, reviewed crew duties, checked our kit and our weapons and then waited. As before, the certainty of our professional competence inspired confidence in our abilities as a crew. Five minutes before we launched, the radio crackled with a check in from the extraction point. It turns out the batteries had died in their radio and they had trouble finding a new set. We redeployed to the UK ten days later, shortly after Laurent Kabila took control of Kinshasa and ousted Mobutu from power.

Women on Operational Deployments

In hindsight, I am truly fortunate to have flown with some of the best pilots, navigators and crewman on both sides of the Atlantic. Conversely, I have also served with some who felt I did not belong in the cockpit of a helicopter, let alone in the cockpit of a tactical helicopter in a war zone. Thankfully, the latter have been few and far between. There is no doubt that, in many ways, operational deployments, and the leadership demands they have placed on me, are different from those experienced by my male counterparts. For most of my career, I have been the lone woman pilot either on squadron or on deployment. Being 'one of' anything generates a great deal of interest in your activities and abilities. Was I there because there was some sort of nebulous quota for women pilots that needed to be filled or did I genuinely merit the wings I wore? That was an added pressure that virtually none of the men I ever flew with had to experience. As I have reiterated throughout the chapter,

I relied on my professional competence to see me through; I knew I could fly and, although I was never the best pilot on the squadron, I was current and qualified and I knew my own limitations.

On those occasions where there were several women pilots, I found myself senior in rank and experience to all of them, a responsibility I did not take lightly. I have never subscribed to the 'I have more experience than you therefore I know everything' school of leadership. Each of these very talented women had their own wisdom and experience and I listened to what they had to say. We tried to schedule girls' nights where we could sit and talk about 'girl stuff' – it was always a much welcomed break from the masculine world we found ourselves in the rest of the time.

I have little experience in operational leadership in a domestic environment having never deployed on a domestic operation. The closest I came was in the UK, several months before I returned to Canada. By this time, with nearly 600 Puma hours under my belt, I had been appointed as a duty authorizer at 33 Sqn, a senior pilot position that entailed a detailed knowledge of the aircraft and the crews since no one could launch until the duty authorizer had approved the flight. I was on duty Easter weekend when torrential flooding across central England prompted a call for Puma support. My beeper sounded at 0400 and I arrived at the squadron shortly thereafter. After reviewing the tasking, I briefed the crew (the aircraft captain was a very senior flight lieutenant who had been one of my instructors three years earlier) and we discussed mission parameters, safety and weather considerations. We also reviewed hoisting procedures as the helicopter was to be fitted with a hoist for this task and it was not standard mission kit for most sorties.

What followed was a rather ugly encounter with the Squadron Commanding Officer (OC) who, having returned home from the mess after a party, arrived at the flight line, still drunk, and attempted to take control of the situation. This individual railed at the maintenance crews for not having the hoist installed yet, berated me for my appearance and proceeded to re-brief the crew, telling them that they were free to break any flight rules they needed to in order to accomplish the mission. I had never been confronted with this type of situation before and, initially, was at a loss as to how to react. In the end, I took the OC outside and asked him to leave the flight line. After doing some name-calling and ranting about exchange officers, he wandered back home. I re-briefed the crew to ensure they were clear on the mission parameters and they subsequently launched on task.

The crew performed admirably and was responsible for rescuing numerous stranded civilians. To the OC's credit, he apologized (once he sobered up), not only to me but to the Puma crew and the maintenance personnel involved in the tasking. Personally, his credibility had been irreparably damaged; however, the incident provided some valuable leadership lessons for me:

1. Every action must exemplify and reinforce your skill as a leader;
2. Exercise good judgment; and
3. Trust your subordinates to get the job done.

Conclusion

I find it interesting that, despite thinking I had little to write on the subject of women, leadership and military operations, I have managed to commit over 6,000 words to paper. I retired from the CF, and from flying, in 2004 and there are few days that go by that I do not miss one or the other. My experiences as a pilot, an officer and a leader, will continue to shape my life and I am grateful for having had them. I would like to think that, in some small way, I set a good example, both as a pilot and an officer, for those women who succeed me and I wish them every success as they partake in, what for me was, a remarkable journey. I'd like to close with words from General J.A. Dextraze, former Canadian Chief of Defence Staff:

> Leadership is self-perpetuating – at least it should be. This means that you, as a leader, have a solemn responsibility to develop leadership in their (sic) subordinates. Remember that all of them sooner or later will have to lead others. The best way you can teach them, of course, is by example, hopefully good example.

ENDNOTES

1   Sun Tzu as excerpted in course notes for the Flying Supervisor's course, 22-25 November 1999.

2   Canada. *Duty with Honour: The Profession of Arms in Canada* (Kingston, ON: Canadian Forces Leadership Institute, 2003), 3 available on-line: http://www.cda-acd.forces.gc.ca/CFLI/engraph/poa/doc/DutyWithHonourLongVers_e.pdf.

3   http://www.dnd.ca/site/reports/somalia/vol1/V1C5_e.asp.

4   Edward R. Murrow, well-known American journalist, as excerpted in course notes for the Flying Supervisor's course, 22-25 November 1999.

5   *Duty with Honour,* 22-23.

6   Ibid., 33.

7   Ibid,, 4.

8   *Canadian Oxford Dictionary*, Second Edition, (Don Mills, ON: Oxford University Press, 2004).

9   2 Canadian Forces Flying Training School.

10   For article given widest distribution see, Weiker, Capt. Sue, "408 in Somalia" *SeaLandAir*. CFB Edmonton 24 (3, March 4, 1993), 1.

11   Excerpted from press information released by Joint Headquarters – OP HAMDEN 3 August 1995.

12   Leptospirosis, an infectious disease that affects humans and animals, is considered the most common zoonosis in the world. Leptospirosis often is referred to as swineherd's disease, swamp fever, or mud fever. After it gains entry via intact skin or mucosa, the organism multiplies in blood and tissue. The resulting leptospiremia can spread to any part of the body but particularly affects the liver and kidney. http://www.emedicine.com/emerg/topic856.htm.

13   In contrast to the 1991 riots in which the population joined the soldiers on a looting spree, the soldiers' rampage in 1993 terrorized the population. Hundreds of civilians were killed, including the French ambassador, Philippe Bernard, who was shot in an attack on the embassy, and the twenty-eight-year-old son of opposition leader Frederic Kibassa Maliba, who was killed during an attack on his father's home. Many more civilians lost their belongings in looting raids conducted by soldiers. There

were numerous reports of rape by soldiers, and the Belgian government claimed that soldiers raped Belgian nuns in the Limete district of Kinshasa. Hundreds of foreigners were evacuated from Kinshasa by French troops; the Belgian troops worked to evacuate foreigners from Brazzaville in neighboring Congo to Europe, because Mobutu refused to allow them into Zaire. http://www.hrw.org/reports/1994/WR94/Africa-10.htm.

14   "A military operation conducted with the aim of ensuring the safe evacuation of non-combatants threatened in a foreign country." AJP – 1A as excerpted from a presentation by Colonel Zimmer, USMC to 33 Sqn RAF in 1997.

15   Temazepam is a short-acting benzodiazepine. It is normally prescribed to people who have difficulty sleeping, or occasionally to reduce anxiety. http://www.urban75.com/Drugs/temazepem.html.

16   As an aside, I experienced extreme fatigue later that year on an exercise in Germany. I had been appointed a Camp Commander for the first few days we were in the field and I had managed only 3 or 4 hours rest each night. I subsequently fell asleep flying straight and level over a city and, on landing, grounded myself for 24 hours. The decision was unpopular amongst the other crews who had to pick up the tasking slack but my confidence in my ability to fly safely was gone. After 24 hours (and about 12 hours of sleep), I returned to flying duties. Months afterwards, there were still those who would make snoring sounds if they saw me in the crew room, but despite these few individuals, I know I made the right decision.

CHAPTER 4

Command at Sea: July 2003 - June 2005

Lieutenant-Commander Marta Mulkins

Almost twenty years ago, the senior strategic leadership of the Canadian Forces (CF) took the decision that sea-going billets in warships would no longer be closed to women (with the exception of submarines, where later restrictions to women were also eventually removed). This was a pragmatic decision that led the institution on a path that better reflected the society which it sought to protect and from which it drew its resources. It was also an act of faith; it presumed that, without institutional barriers, women would eventually command ships and by extension possibly even the Navy itself. This act catalysed institutional and environmental change with the goal of improving effectiveness and collective performance. In this case, the Navy sought to maintain its high professional standard while now better reflecting Canadian society and values as a whole.

Thanks in part to this decision, on 11 July 2003, I assumed command of HMCS (Her Majesty's Canadian Ship) *Kingston* and embarked on two of the most challenging – and rewarding – years of my life. Personally gratifying as it is for all who attain it, events on that day received a bit more attention because I was the first woman in the Canadian Navy to command a ship. As can be imagined, through the following two years my ship and I were subject to slightly different scrutiny and assessment on a variety of levels; unconscious, casual, deliberate or official. While this scrutiny and associated judgement by others never caused any particular anxiety, it was an ever-present factor, which, even when it was benign or even well intentioned, likely cast the complexion of my command in a slightly different light than that of my male peers. Recognizing that other women in similar circumstances will likely experience the same type of interest in their progress, I hope that sharing my experiences will offer evidence that it need not be negative; we live in an era of firsts for women, both within the military and in our society as a whole and the scrutiny need not be daunting if it engages the interest of a wider audience. In this chapter I will briefly describe the responsibilities of command at sea and the path to reaching the qualification, and offer some impressions of how different factors may have affected how I and my ship's company built a strong and effective team despite being 'under the microscope'.

In Pursuit of Command at Sea

HMCS *Kingston* is one of twelve coastal patrol ships operated by the Navy. The Kingston class of ships is based on a typical mine-warfare platform, similar in dimension, tonnage and equipment to other navies' minesweepers. The ships are tasked with a range of missions including general coastal patrols, search-and-rescue zone and sovereignty patrols, fisheries patrols supporting Department of Fisheries and Oceans and smuggling prevention patrols supporting the Royal Canadian Mounted Police (RCMP). On the west coast, these ships also conduct submarine escort/force protection duties. They perform a variety of mine warfare tasks including route survey using side-scan sonar and bottom-object inspection with remotely operated vehicles. Kingston class ships participate in NATO mine warfare exercises off the coast of Europe and fleet exercises off Norfolk and Hawaii every few years. The platform is used to train Reserve and Regular Force Navy officers, and reserve tradesmen and women. The ships are lightly armed. They carry a ship's company of 32 to 47, depending on the mission. While the crew is a mix of Reserve and Regular Force Navy, the majority are reserves. Based on the size and armament, they are deemed 'minor warships'; to qualify to command one, a Maritime Surface (MARS) officer in the Navy must: write a series of exams proving knowledge of all systems, procedures and operations; complete a specified period of time in rank; serve for a period as the Executive Officer (second-in-command) in a minor warship; and finally successfully complete an oral and simulator-based examination called the Minor Warship Command Board. Major warships, including frigates, destroyers and replenishment ships, require a commanding officer to have passed the Major Warship Command Board. No woman has yet commanded a major warship, though at least one is qualified to do so at this time.

Having passed the Minor Warship board in the fall of 2000, I was determined that, having gone through years of hard work to achieve the qualification, it would be only a partial success if I did not put the qualification to use; the proof would be in the doing. Throughout this progress toward the goal of Command at Sea, I was increasingly aware that I would likely be the first woman to win the job; the 'first' aside, it was one of my stronger wishes that my ship not be singled out for any further unusual attention – either positive or negative. All other factors being equal, it was very important to me that the ship not receive – or perhaps even more importantly, not be seen to receive, different taskings or be held to different standards – in short, to receive different treatment because of the single fact of who was in command. The notion that my ship's company might ever suffer because I was their captain was a deeply discouraging concept for me. Treatment with impartiality was not only important for the ship itself, but also for the maintenance of a normal rapport with our sister ships.

That said, the events surrounding my appointment and assumption of command had some irregularities. I had been unofficially assessed by the senior Commander of the Operations Group in a tacit 'check ride' of sorts while still an Executive Officer. Following the presumably successful examination, I received the message that I had been appointed to command of HMCS *Kingston* twenty-four hours before the Change-of-Command ceremony was to occur. While the Navy's official stance on all women's achievements now is essentially one of 'no big deal – she is succeeding in line with her male peers', a local television crew was permitted to film the ceremony. During my first weeks in the job, I gave a number of television interviews and indeed throughout my two years in command was frequently interviewed by media. None of this was onerous and indeed it seemed that the media generally treated it as a positive story. Most importantly to me, it felt that the fairness and objectivity from the chain of command, the staff, my peers and colleagues for which I hoped, had in fact transpired. For the most part, the institution seemed to work.

Throughout that time, the ship accomplished a range of missions: including two deployments to the Great Lakes, participating in a number of search-

and rescue missions, exercising at different times with the Canadian East Coast Task Group and the Standing NATO Task Group, successfully completing the at-sea competency check of a 'Work-Up', training numerous junior officers, qualifying many new tradespeople, conducting route survey operations and fisheries patrols, and executing trials in support of developing new coastal defence technologies. The general consensus on that period in HMCS *Kingston* (18 months), and HMCS *Summerside* (six months) was that it was a success; we accomplished all missions with what seemed to me strong professionalism and generally good cheer. In my departure address to the ship's company, I told them I thought our greatest strength was our will to do well whatever we undertook. We were a very good team. I write this with humility because we all know too well how a single stroke of sheer bad luck can affect the reputations of highly skilled and respected commanders; we certainly encountered our share of incidents, but none was outside of our control or ability to resolve; we suffered no real bad luck.

The alternative, however, would have potentially had great repercussions beyond the bruising of a single ego or reputation; at best, those who doubted the outcome of my appointment but had remained quiet pending some excuse to say 'I told you so' likely would have not hesitated to do so; at worst, it could have been for a long while held up as an example not of the failure of an individual but of generalized failure of all women – and could have marred the hope of women far more talented than I to have a chance to succeed in the near future.

This chapter represents my initial attempt to analyse factors that permitted my period in command to remain relatively normal despite the extra pressures of expectation, scrutiny and judgement. Given the experience I now have and the chance to command at sea again, my approach to some issues would certainly be different; there are most definitely some issues which I believe I could have handled much better than I did. If nothing else, the account of my own experience may be interesting or even reassuring to someone who finds herself in a similar situation, identifying in her own experience the same leadership factors and techniques (conscious or otherwise) that enabled me to keep HMCS *Kingston* and the Navy off the front page of the *Globe and Mail* for all the wrong reasons.

Leadership Concepts

One of the primary references for leadership theory in the Canadian Forces is *Leadership in the Canadian Forces: Conceptual Foundations.* In laying out a framework for the systematic analysis of the components of leadership, it proposes that 'leader power' is divided into two components: 'position power', which is the authority conferred simply by virtue of position or rank, and 'personal power' which is gained or lost through the exercise of "…socially valued or useful qualities of an individual."[1] It stresses that both may be transitory, position power being attached to the appointment and therefore ending with the appointment. Personal power may be maintained, but depends on the favourable reception by others of one's personality traits. Most importantly, the reference reminds us:

> Because power is an attribution made by others, and because leaders cannot control how others perceive and interpret their behaviour, leaders have to be mindful of the fact that they are always 'on parade' and that their conduct and performance will add to, or detract from their power credits…[2]

The analyst of a leadership experience, therefore must, according to the reference, ask certain questions, including the following:

1. Did the leader find the right balance between 'position power' and 'personal power'?; and

2. Did the subordinates reward the leadership with a 'committed' response to his or her direction?

The question of achieving the right balance of 'position' and 'personal' powers resonates immediately to anyone in a leadership position – it is the essence of the issue. Did the team follow orders and direction because they could not avoid it – or because they understood and believed in what they were doing?

Perhaps the product of long-ago leadership theory training in basic training, certainly honed by years of being one of few women in leadership roles in the various ships and units in which I served, it seemed obvious to me that, while success in leading the ship would be due to a balance between the two, it was more important to maintain strong 'personal power'. Anyone deserving of command (or any position of leadership) can be so appointed, and the ship's company would follow orders because the military assigns the commander legitimate authority over them – but the "I do what she says because I have to," and the coercive component implied by that response to authority would hardly support this 'proof of concept', particularly under the ubiquitous microscope. Few opinions in a ship are more important than those of the unofficial leaders in the junior ranks' mess – and nothing travels outside of a ship faster to set our reputation among our peers. To lead effectively – whether under the scrutiny of others or not – my personal competence, conduct and consideration of others had to earn the crew's respect and trust. They had to feel that I was credible to my superiors (in order to better represent and defend us when required), that I had integrity, and was motivated for the right reasons. Combined with this, my personal belief and enthusiasm for our tasks and missions, correctly explained to the ship, went a long way to gaining sustained commitment in return from them. While every leader will state the obvious desire to achieve commitment, I believe that its importance was elevated for HMCS *Kingston*; fortunately I think it was mostly, if not entirely, achieved.

Leading People

How then, did the ship succeed as it did – how was the team prepared at the outset, how did we evolve through our collective experience and how were we then better prepared to handle setbacks? In other words, what were the group capabilities that permitted us to be as reliable and as resilient as possible?

From time to time, people with no experience in the military would ask me how I could have exercised authority in my ship, clearly assuming that I should have had 'problems with the guys'. In reassuring them that I did not (and for that matter, that I never had throughout my career in the Reserve), I found it surprisingly difficult to make them understand that these were not rank, undisciplined kids crewing these ships, and that the discipline, professionalism and overriding importance of the team were the hallmarks of any CF unit. While the gap between their image of the military and the actual reality was a bit alarming, these interactions served to remind me of that which we ultimately have to take for granted in the CF – that authority will be respected, order maintained and professionalism is the norm. Clearly, the training system that produced these individuals deserves the first mention in answering how the team came to be as capable as it was.

Of note, and clear testament to their own excellent leadership, was the instant and unquestioning support offered to me from the other two members of the Command Team, the Executive Officer and the Coxswain. Their influence on the ship's company was immeasurable; undoubtedly through their attitude and tone, they transmitted a positive anticipation and expectation. Had they shown anything less then the utmost support to me from the first day onward, it would certainly have made my first days in the new job more difficult. This positive atmosphere probably made the team more receptive when I explained my philosophies and expectations to set the tone for the ship. It was made clear that I expected the highest standards of professionalism, and in turn would strive to give them every opportunity to advance; I stressed my approach to issues would be 'firm but fair' and that while we would work very hard, we would certainly play hard as well. In what was probably the only time I addressed the elephant in the room, I stated that I would do whatever I could to shield them from any extra attention that might be aimed at me. Beyond that, I believe I deliberately did not again acknowledge the scrutiny we were all under – hopefully relegating the obvious to 'minor inconvenience' status. It is possible though that the Executive Officer and the Coxswain may have kept that factor in mind in their own direction to the team.

The ship soon thereafter received a number of small but significant challenges – scheduled or otherwise – which served to build our cohesion, sense of capability and *esprit de corps*. These so-called 'small triumphs'[3]– which included some engineering emergencies, a search-and-rescue for downed United States Marine Corps (USMC) F-18 pilots, a hurricane and being chosen for a particularly tough sea trial appropriately nicknamed 'slamming trials' – built our collective resilience and pride. In some sense, we were lucky to have been in the right place at the right time. This stood us in good stead for the previously mentioned work-up and other tests of our capabilities.

Of all the ways in which I was able to influence our ship's performance however, I believe the most important was in the direct and uncompromising expression of the military ethos I expected, which was subsequently reinforced through words and deeds throughout the two years. Just as I had felt that HMCS *Kingston* had to be 'committed' in accomplishing all missions, we also had to meet the highest expectation of professionalism. I believe this philosophy, clearly communicated and reinforced, served us well.

Considerations

Notwithstanding all the accomplishments by women in Canadian society, some people still, openly or otherwise, remain skeptical about women's capabilities to perform military roles. There is the seemingly deep-seated suspicion that women will be unable to carry their own weight in combat situations. Despite evidence across all the services of women's successes in military roles, pundits still like to call up images such as that of pulling an injured comrade out of the field as proof that women should not be in combat roles. These opinions ignore the role women already play in similar trades and professions such as law enforcement and expects us to accept, as proof, selected examples of women's failures in other countries and cultures, some of which are very different from our own and have little to no relevance to our own experience. Most perplexing of all is the tendency to completely ignore both the institutional successes in integrating women and the specific achievements of individuals, writing them off as statistical anomalies, supposedly meaningless within the big picture. This betrays a deep misunderstanding of what integration has meant for the CF; an insistence that it is a social engineering experiment which forces people into roles to which they are fundamentally unsuited, rather than the simple removal of artificial barriers to those who have the ability to succeed, supporting the notion that 'those who can, will'.

For obvious reasons then, it likely helps women in uniform to manage how they are perceived both by their peers and by those outside of the CF, though this is not intended to make women feel unnecessarily self-conscious. It is beneficial to have, for lack of a better way to express it, a 'physical presence' in the sense that, not only does one have to be fit, but it helps immensely to also be seen to be fit, to be making the effort to be strong enough not only to carry one's own weight, but to be a viable contributor to the team as a whole. In any case, in my experience, life in a ship ironically requires a rather different form of physical resilience and endurance. Comments about physical strength are much reduced when reminded that, at sea, there is an equal-opportunity disabler that levels the playing field between men, women, the great and the small: sea sicknesses. It does not discriminate, and can fell the most physically robust while not affecting others; it is the great equalizer. While a lot of muscle power heaving on the lines on the upper decks or in sawing lumber for damage control shoring is appreciated, it cannot and does not determine overall ability at sea in a modern warship.

Conclusion

Canadian history is starred with the actions of women, some of which have proven pivotal in the various conflicts of our nation's building. It is not well enough known that women in Canada have participated in the military since serving during the Northwest Rebellion in 1885 and since then have continued to make significant advances in the substance of participation, including taking part in combat in the 1991 Gulf War, in keeping with women's advances throughout Canadian society as a whole. As can be imagined, it was important that the faith the CF had in the ultimate ability of women to succeed at sea was proven not to be misguided or merely 'politically correct'. The degree of risk it assumed is a debate in its own right; the bottom line is that without the eventual appointment of women to senior positions in competition with their (male and female) peers, the decision may have been discounted as mistaken, empty, or at worst, delusional. It therefore ultimately meant that women in leadership positions, including commanding at the tactical level would also, through the simple act of their leadership, actually be completing a strategic goal. Either end of the leadership spectrum, from the strategic decision-maker to the tactical commander at sea, meets in the middle to change the institution.

Even now, the notion expressed in the reference that leaders are always 'on parade' remains true for me. I know that some people will always assess my behaviour against their individual notion of 'what is a captain' – perhaps I may have altered their point of view in this regard. I hope this study provides some illumination into my own leadership approach, which will likely continue to guide me in future roles and opportunities. Though we remain in anticipation of a woman assuming command of a major warship, I am confident that that fortunate woman will be met with a most positive reception. A woman commanding a ship in the Canadian Navy is no longer a hurdle to be overcome, though one must never underestimate the numbers of individuals who must still actually see in order to believe. In any case, Canada is back in step with fellow western nations that were already beyond the issue, and a signal has been sent to Canadians that their Navy is a fair and representative institution. Perhaps most importantly, all Canadians can be reassured that they will be given every opportunity to succeed, that being the greatest gift of all.

ENDNOTES

1   Department of National Defence, *Leadership in the Canadian Forces: Conceptual Foundations* (Ottawa: CDA, Canadian Forces Leadership Institute, 2005), 58.

2   Ibid., 59.

3   Ibid., 79.

CHAPTER 5

"There's No Hell Like Tac Hel!"

Major Jamie Speiser-Blanchet

Leadership is a broad topic that has existed and evolved since the beginning of time. My experience has been encouraging, in that the Canadian Forces (CF) has offered a vast variety of leadership opportunities. Every occupation deals with different techniques, approaches and experiences with leadership that clearly underline the never-ending opportunities for individuals to learn and develop. For the military occupation of pilot, for instance, an officer may spend many years perfecting the technical knowledge and piloting skills required to operate before being in a position with actual subordinates, which normally occurs at the rank of senior captain or major. The leadership learned and developed in those formative years is perhaps less obvious than a classical definition would suggest, but it is no less critical to the organization and the successful accomplishment of military duties. This leadership deals less with direct supervision techniques and responsibilities, but does require vital teambuilding skills in a crew concept environment while dealing with highly skilled individuals in all aspects of the flying community.

Women are particularly well suited to this interactive, team-oriented environment, where communication and teamwork are vital to the success of the mission. My experience as a female tactical helicopter (tac hel) pilot has taken me on numerous missions abroad and domestically, and the skills developed throughout my career so far have taught me much about the integrity, professionalism and stamina required of Canadian military leaders today. However, it has done so through a leadership experience that has differed significantly from my counterparts in other environments. My own personality and outlook have allowed me to embrace tremendous leadership opportunities and apply them in my work as an officer and pilot, whether deployed or in garrison. With a very challenging environment of change upon us for the foreseeable future, it is an especially important time for effective leadership in the CF at all levels and I believe everyone can benefit from sharing experiences with others.

As I look back on the paths taken that led me to where I am today, I see that there have always been issues unique to me as a female in the non-traditional world of the military and tactical aviation. As a single woman, certain issues set me apart from my male counterparts and now, married with two young children, the issues have changed but a basic premise remains constant: being a woman with different goals, a different role at home and a different physiological composition is still all that sets me apart from the men I work with. What is essential to understand is that these issues have not prevented me from integrating and succeeding in my chosen environment as a military tac hel pilot, they have simply taught me about myself and have led me to be more aware of the effects of personal, human factors among my peers and subordinates. This understanding of human nature is very powerful in that it is integral in the process of developing and motivating any team, where the inspiration of confidence in followers or the leadership is arguably crucial to the success of any mission.

Leadership is a vast topic and the basic premise of influencing others to do one's will entails many variables on how best to achieve this goal. I personally view effective leadership as the clear communication of the team or organisation's vision and mission as the team is guided toward a goal. An effective leader will set an honest example and provide a challenging environment where subordinates and team members can develop and reach their own potential. This view can be applied to a team as small as a helicopter crew or maintenance section, to an entire squadron, wing or larger magnitude. Officers, by virtue of their profession, have the responsibility to uphold certain values, such as honesty and loyalty, as they set an example, whether their actions influence peers, subordinates or even supervisors. As a woman in the very male environment of tactical aviation, I have personally and professionally thrived, as I have had many opportunities for learning and growth that have taught me not only about leadership values, but the overwhelming importance of seeking to understand others and what motivates them. Through my experiences deployed and at home, I have discovered some interesting facets that may help other leaders understand the women and men working with them.

Having begun my military career at the Royal Military College of Canada (RMC) studying computer engineering before undergoing pilot training in Moose Jaw and Portage La Prairie, I have always been one of few females in my environment. My first posting, to 430e Escadron tactique d'hélicoptères in Valcartier, introduced me to the operational world of tactical helicopters and included peacekeeping deployments to Haiti and Bosnia in addition to support to several domestic operations, such as relief for forest fires in Chibougamau, Saguenay Floods, the Ice Storm in Québec and the Summit of the Americas. As an operational tactical aviation squadron, much of our flying involved working with the Army in order to provide support in the form of transportation, surveillance, and reconnaissance, among other utility tasks. Again, with no subordinates, the leadership developed during this time involved small three or four person crews as I progressed from First Officer to Aircraft Captain, which signified a substantial increase in responsibility and accountability as I learned to plan and carry out more complex missions. The aircraft captain is essentially responsible for all aspects of the aircraft and mission and directs or leads the crew, including a flight engineer, as required. In addition to carrying out regular piloting duties at an operational squadron, several pilots are required to hold key positions that may entail the supervision of others or the management of resources, so this also contributes to a pilot's learning experience.

This posting was followed by a staff tour in Operations at 1 Wing Headquarters in Kingston, where I learned a great deal about the importance of effective communication of assigned goals and directives and gained a more global view of the role of tactical aviation squadrons in Canada. Currently posted to 403 (Helicopter) Operational Training Squadron as the Operations Officer, I am directly responsible for the coordination of all Squadron taskings, which primarily entails, but is not limited to, pilot and flight engineer training on the Griffon helicopter. I command a flight of thirty personnel who assist me in managing the flying operations, air traffic control, readiness training and information systems management and I continue to learn more about leadership every day. My current position requires a great deal of negotiating and coordinating of information in order to accomplish unit goals and I have learned the importance of tact and direct communication. Now a senior officer, the lessons I have learned from operating at the tactical and operational planning levels have also been very valuable and have influenced my current approach to supervising and leading my operations team.

My career progression throughout all my postings and deployments has resulted from a work ethic that does not allow me to accept less than my full effort on any task or assignment. My strategy has simply been to accomplish all goals in a way I think they should be done, as openly as possible, with feedback and communication to everyone directly related to the task at hand. I have never had the need for hidden agendas or special projects to demonstrate potential; I took on projects of interest and helped others when I could, feeling quite capable of saying no when my plate was too full. I feel it is very important to learn from others, and while this concept of openly sharing experiences may not come easily to some and may be considered a very feminine trait by others, it has allowed me to personally glean vast amounts of knowledge from all kinds of contacts. Whether it is a lesson learned on how not to act in a given situation, or an example of exceptional leadership ability, every individual has something to offer if you are open to learning it.

I have a natural desire to succeed and an aversion to failure, which gets the better of me sometimes, and is perhaps more accurately labelled as perfectionism. Ironically, I do know that perfection is not realistic and I am very aware that I have much to learn no matter how much I know. This trait continues to develop and hopefully always will. I also have what I consider to be a certain amount of naivety when it comes to the organization and my contribution to it; I cannot help but believe that I can make a difference somewhere, though I have seen often enough how even the best-staffed intentions or suggestions cannot survive budget cuts, resource constraints or general lack of motivation for the increased workload initially required to reach a better state. And yet I hold on to the belief that we can always improve the system in some way and that motivated and balanced leaders are required at all levels of the chain of command. All in all, my approach to my career has been a very open and personal one and I strive to ensure my behaviour and attitude do not change whether I am dealing with subordinates, peers or supervisors. While I may have held back in the early stages of my career, acting or not acting in a way that would not draw attention to myself as a rare woman, I have let go of any preconceived notions about what others may think of me and I am very transparent in my approach now as a senior officer. I would argue that a certain confidence is necessary to allow this freedom of expression, but this has come from the feeling that my opinions have been respected and listened to along the way and that I have no reason to hold back when I have a contribution to make. This has not only been important to my personal philosophy, but I encourage this attitude in all those I work with or lead, either in the cockpit or the office environment.

Managing dwindling resources in addition to people makes leadership in today's military even more challenging. I have found that individuals are faced with more stress with shorter timelines for projects and there is a constant demand for results within every organization I have been a part of. In tactical aviation, not unlike other areas, the community has recently faced multiple deployments with reduced numbers of personnel and this places a significant burden on families and the members themselves. This instability can be demoralizing for someone who then becomes very reactive to unforeseen and frequent changes so I strive to mitigate this effect by communicating expectations as much as possible with peers and subordinates. This can be surprisingly difficult with the vast amounts of information we deal with given modern technology. It has become challenging for supervisors to get away from e-mails to speak face to face with subordinates and still manage the constant throughput of taskings. As a supervisor and pilot, much time is typically spent in the aircraft, so there is an added pressure to accomplish staff work with less office time. I personally rely on peers and other supervisors who are working with me as they often provide good advice and offer useful sounding boards for ideas.

As the first female pilot at my initial posting at 430 Squadron, I was thrust into a tightly knit group of men who shared close social ties in addition to professional ones. Although not the first female tactical aviator in the aviation community as a whole; I was the first at this squadron. I attribute my ability to become a valued part of this team to my own optimistic attitude, but also largely to the maturity and positive attitudes of the men I worked with. While my presence required some shifting in their accepted culture and behaviour, it was perhaps not seen as such a monumental change since the Air Force teamwork climate allowed for a positive attitude toward change and the integration of women, despite the non-traditional role. Most of the time, I felt that I was assessed based on my actions rather than my gender or the possible preconceived notions others may have had. The chauvinistic male attitudes have fortunately been few and far between in my experience. In most cases, I chose to see past the usually gruff, macho exteriors of these men to the misguided insecurities beneath, and I learned to let unwarranted negative comments go. I have always tried to promote the presence of women in the aviation community, either by encouraging young women at recruiting events or during the many media interviews I have been involved in. I have often been asked why there are so few women in my field and my honest opinion is that women must not know about the opportunities that exist for them in aviation. This fact is changing, but very slowly, as the number of female pilots in the CF is still quite low, amounting to about two percent of the total.

This ability of my co-workers to accept a woman into their group was not something I saw universally, though I feel the CF continues to make tremendous progress every day. While the Air Force had begun to evolve in the acceptance of women in non-traditional roles when I went through my pilot training and first posting, I noticed that my female counterparts within the army and navy seemed to face harsher judges, a fact I believe was related to the differences in the social cultures between the environments and the nature of our missions: an Air Force team, even when working closely with the Army as in tactical aviation, requires cooperation and team support to get aircraft in the air while the army arguably requires a more direct response to orders in order to accomplish some of their elementary tasks. Their tasks are generally more physical than most air force tasks as well, and being a woman never presented an insurmountable physical challenge for me within the Air Force.

With more women filling non-traditional roles in our military today and the open attitude of a younger generation, there is much wider acceptance of the female presence because it is simply more common and represents to me a very logical progression that was simply stifled in the past by societal norms. The characteristics that set me apart as a woman are not directly related to my performance, which is in my opinion why women can integrate so well into certain military environments. The issues that made us different were more personal in nature, and I believe it is simply a respect and understanding of the fact that women bring different emotional and personal baggage to the table than men that can allow a supervisor to be more in tune with the needs of his or her subordinates and peers, and thus more effectively lead any team, simply because understanding and allowing individual expression within a team can only enhance a leader's ability to employ individual capabilities to accomplish a mission.

I have always been one of only a few females in my cohort throughout my education, training and subsequent career. As such, I remember learning to deal with perception issues and coping with some form of the ubiquitous spotlight that followed the women wherever we went. I saw a choice early in my career that I could either accept the attention and learn to coexist with it peacefully, or I could let it eat at me and slowly erode my self-confidence and peace of mind. This was, I believe, my greatest challenge as a female leader adjusting to a male culture, for even though I chose the co-existence option, it was not always easy to ignore that I could not blend in and go unnoticed for long. The feeling that any mistake you make will be attributed to all the other women that follow your footsteps may sound extreme, but it was a very real perception to me, whether at RMC as a young officer cadet in training or as a new pilot embarking on an exciting career. This feeling dissipates with experience and maturity, but never quite disappears. The attention I garnered as the only female pilot on deployments was the main point that set my experience apart from the men's. Image management can then become very important since all actions are scrutinized and widely noticed in an environment where speculation, rumours and loneliness abound. My own approach to this situation was to let it go as much as possible, while staying true to my own personality and values. I relied heavily on my good friends, mostly male, and we all supported each other.

During my first peacekeeping operation, in Haiti, I deployed as a lieutenant and very newly trained Griffon pilot. As such, I had no subordinates, but worked very closely with my peers in a crew concept environment. With the overall mission of contributing to a secure and stable environment in Haiti for the United Nations (UN), our actual helicopter missions were quite varied and allowed us to interact with personnel from other countries as we transported mainly UN troops to remote areas on the island that were not easily accessible by land. As the only female pilot and one of very few women on the camp, the biggest challenge I faced was that of dealing with the attention garnered as a result of my minority status and the ensuing challenge to ensure it did not affect my job performance and mission accomplishment. It was obviously a new situation for many of my supervisors and peers and it was indeed challenging for all to adjust to my presence. Some were concerned with the perception of preferential treatment, for example, when I was given a room of my own since I could not be lodged with the other male pilots; this was not in fact a big deal for most of my coworkers, but showed that there were special administrative considerations required because I was the only woman. At that point in my career it was indeed an additional source of stress; I worried about what others thought and did not want extra attention. I most certainly did not want anyone to think I received special treatment, and I in fact spent several weeks on dreaded standby status without complaint when a fellow pilot commented to supervisors that I had more flying hours than the other co-pilots. I learned quickly that perception, even when inaccurate, can have very real consequences.

On my subsequent tour with NATO in Bosnia, I was the only female in the entire helicopter detachment and with more experience by this time, was appointed Adjutant in addition to my piloting duties. Challenged by a stimulating, mine-filled area of flying operations, I appreciated the opportunity to learn more about such an historical part of the world. Faced with more responsibility as Adjutant, I found this experience helpful in preparing me for future professional challenges as it allowed me to develop a great deal of confidence in my staff work and piloting skills. I had the good fortune of working with an excellent supervisor who provided me with opportunities to reach my full potential professionally while allowing me to grow as a person. He did not care that I was the only female and proved that my gender was simply not important when it came to job performance and effectiveness; he assigned me tasks that were important to the well-being of others and displayed the utmost confidence in my abilities. The position of adjutant did not come with actual subordinates, but was significant to the detachment since I was directly responsible for administration, discipline issues and the ever popular leave plan for all members of the detachment. As such, my actions had a direct impact on the morale of the members of all sections, not just the aircrew.

Maintaining morale for all personnel is of crucial importance during a six-month deployment where such things as phone calls, e-mails and regular mail can represent a real lifeline from loved ones back home. Getting to know the other members of the detachment and living through the roller coaster of emotions that can accompany a deployment really allowed me to learn about human nature and dealing with a wide range of behaviours. I have found that women, in general, can be more intuitive when helping others work through emotional problems than most men (with exceptions of course). My approach to problem solving comes naturally to me because I value the importance of listening to someone and validating their feelings, even before trying to tackle the issue at hand. I noticed that some men would try to solve a perceived problem that actually diffused itself as soon as an individual had the chance to talk and be heard, and that most men do not often wish to express their feelings, certainly not as women do. While on deployment, communication and listening become even more meaningful, and can greatly affect morale and unit cohesiveness.

Both deployments taught me about coping with loneliness and distance, but also about keeping a positive attitude despite challenging conditions.

Some key elements stood out as I learned to deal with life as a woman on a military deployment; while we are all arguably different, I found that I shared some unique traits with the other women I deployed with, even if they were of other occupations or units. These were primarily the need for communication and emotional expression, a strong sense of community and the sharing of common experiences. I was definitely more emotional than the men I worked with, meaning that I expressed my feelings (e.g. happiness, loneliness, frustration) differently, often by inadvertently wearing them on my sleeve. As someone whose emotions are usually readily apparent, I learned to become conscious of how my attitude could affect others and I learned very quickly that I could not change my personality to suit anyone's expectations. I chose to feel comfortable in just being myself, though I was initially quite self-conscious. Letting go of what others think is not always easy for someone in a new situation, male or female, and for a minority who stands out it can be quite challenging; over time I came to accept that I could not control what others thought of me and decided to simply remain true to my own values.

In a serious relationship during my deployment to Haiti, but single when deployed to Bosnia, my emotional experiences during these tours differed significantly. As a single woman on deployments or missions, the loneliness was perhaps the greatest emotional challenge. Attention was never lacking for any of the few females on the army camps in Haiti and Bosnia, but getting noticed as a minority was nothing new to me, and did not compensate for the absence of loved ones. I relished the friendships I made with my co-workers, and was especially thankful for those forged with other women on deployment with me. That camaraderie was, and is, an important part of coping with the distance from loved ones and loneliness. Years later when my fiancée deployed to Bosnia, I also experienced a deployment as the spouse at home and actually found that experience to be the most difficult of the three. This was mainly because I found the routine when deployed in theatre to be initially very new and exciting, with several challenges that allowed for the time to pass quickly. At home the routine does not change, except that the partner is missing from the usual activities, leaving a void that must be managed.

Another trait shared by most women I encountered was the desire to improve our living environment and to be involved in the community, no matter how austere. This is a characteristic that many men share as well, but I found the proportional number of women involved in group activities like sports, clubs or humanitarian projects to be quite significant. I believed very strongly, as did most men and women on deployment, in using fitness to battle stress and fatigue, as it proved to indeed be a significant morale booster and worthwhile pastime. Women seek comfort in sharing, participating and communicating with others, and this is a very valuable point for any leader to understand, as it can actually have an effect on the rest of a unit. It was very heart-warming to see how many men reluctantly got involved in various activities at the encouragement of the women, only to recognize the power to distract from the isolation as their enthusiasm towards these events grew.

While on these deployments, I was struck by what my friends with children at home lived through. Now a mother, I can empathize even more, because the idea of leaving my child for six months is extremely disturbing. I have not yet experienced a deployment away from my children, but expect to face it at some point in my career and I look back in awe at the mothers I deployed with who lived through the experience. It is difficult enough for a father to be away from his family, but for a mother, I find there is an added sense of responsibility to be with the children. The age of the children will greatly affect the family dynamic, of course, but I don't think it is ever easy. Deployed mothers lived through lessons I have since learned simply as a working mother: communication is in every way a lifeline and sanity maintainer, sharing with others living through a similar experience is vital, and the support of a loving partner is essential. These are views that I feel apply even to the single members on deployment, but they are amplified significantly for all parents, amplified immeasurably for mothers.

Luckily, the majority of my peers were very supportive, always respectful and even somewhat protective, treating me much like a little sister on many occasions. The friendships I formed with those men are still strong years later and the mutual respect is still very present. These relationships spanned all types of deployments, even domestic operations like support to floods and the ice storm, or on exercises with the army, where I was still the only female in our group, a fact that never went unnoticed by others we worked with. Professionally, I have met with little resistance to my presence as a female officer and pilot. Culturally, it was fascinating to see the differences between Canada's military and those of other countries whose military does not include women. In Haiti, the Pakistani soldiers, quite incredulous and sceptical at first, were captivated by the fact that a woman would be flying the helicopter, and actually asked to confirm no less than five times who exactly was flying the mission. Like other organizations unaccustomed to seeing women in my role, even Canadian Army troops, they seemed to accept that I was qualified and capable and were quick to embrace the idea so that it was not problematic.

While my overall career experience has been extremely positive, there was a time when I did want to give up. The instability of a military lifestyle can be very demanding, even on single members, and ups and downs are quite normal. The biggest low in my life and career was emotionally driven and resulted from the fact that I believed my career choice to have a devastating impact on the attainment of my personal goals and dreams. The turning point for me came from the actions of an exceptional and understanding leader I worked for. At my lowest emotional point, I was an unhappy single woman in a male environment, struggling with the perceived loss of my dreams of happiness, profound loneliness and an annoying spotlight that continued to plague me. This was fairly early in my career, during my first posting, when I was still learning to deal with the attention I received as the only female. I initially fought the fact that I was different from the men with boundless stamina, even though I had different personal goals and some unique physical requirements that just couldn't be ignored in the field or on deployments. I did not find consolation with my male friends and felt quite alone after a significant break-up.

Experience will teach anyone that relationships and heartbreak are a normal part of life and they seem trivial to many, but for one to truly understand others as a leader should seek to do, one needs to comprehend that these emotions are very real at the time, no matter how temporary. My motivation to fly and continue my career was greatly decreased by my disillusionment at that time, and this is something I can now recognize in others now that I am the supervisor. To balance the appropriate amount of respect for other's feelings with the needs of the organisation is, I believe, one of the biggest challenges for leaders today. My Flight Commander validated my feelings during this emotionally turbulent time, allowing me to feel that is was okay to share them. Ironically, I did not really wish to do so because I was the only woman and mostly wanted to forget that fact and the loneliness I felt as a result. But this man, an exceptional leader from whom I have learned many lessons, somehow recognized that I would respond to a challenge and assigned me important responsibilities during our deployment to Bosnia, rather than allow me to continue feeling sorry for myself. By not taking an inhumane "get over it and on with it" type of approach that I have seen some leaders adopt, he allowed me to discover strength in myself, which eventually led me to discover that my happiness did not depend on my surroundings or a meaningful partner, but on my own attitude and personal choices.

Involved in this healing process was the realisation that I actually was different from the men. While not a staggering epiphany to most, it was this simple realization that allowed me to find harmony with respect to my situation. Being different did not have to be a bad thing. Instead of beating my head against a wall fighting an obvious fact, I chose to embrace the fact that I was different and celebrate what those differences allowed me to contribute to the organization at all levels. I chose not to feel self-conscious of the spotlight; I could feel proud of my accomplishments, learn from my mistakes and actually try to set an example to others. As the pressure I had inadvertently allowed to weigh me down dissipated, so too did my perception of the spotlight fade. It has never fully departed, but my changing attitude toward it has allowed me the peace of mind important to a happy soul. I found constancy in just being true to myself and bringing my own personality and gifts to every situation. As a leader, I maintain this attitude toward subordinates, peers and superiors that I deal with, for I truly believe everyone has unique qualities that can contribute meaningfully to any team when explored to their full potential.

Now as a senior officer and new mother with another baby on the way, I feel it is very important to learn from all my experiences thus far and apply them to every aspect of my life. Leadership is an ever-evolving skill and I truly believe we never stop learning. To that end, it will always remain crucial that leaders share their knowledge and experience with others. I have had the good fortune of sharing unforgettable memories with many people during my tac hel piloting career at home and abroad, and I cherish their contributions to my life experience. A strong believer of constant learning from any possible source, I am thankful for the varied leadership opportunities I have been presented and look forward to applying them not only to the ever-changing environment of Canadian tactical aviation, but also to the evolution of our military as a whole.

CHAPTER 6

Canadian Forces "MAMS" – Mobile Air Mobility Support – Women Traffic Technicians at Work on Domestic and Deployed Operations

Major Deanna Manson

Traffic Technicians (Traffic Techs) are known best by the burly nature of their profession and have a reputation for being among the hardest working souls both at work and at play. The trade was first opened to women in 1976, although at that time their employment was limited to administrative functions such as furniture and effects clerks, shipping and receiving clerks, and passenger booking system operators. The more labour-intensive side of the trade on line crews, Mobile Air Mobility Support (MAMS) teams and loadmaster employment came later in the 1980s. Today, they work side-by-side their male counterparts, whether it be pushing ten thousand pound pallets onto an aircraft or operating material and ground-handling vehicles of every shape and description. The representation of women in the Traffic Tech trade today is comparable to most support trades in the Canadian Forces (CF), with 143 women comprising 21 percent.[1]

Like many women in the CF, the women in the Traffic Tech trade are most interested in doing their job to the best of their ability. In spite of the widespread reluctance to be singled out because they are women, special thanks is extended to those who took part in the preparation of this article: Major Christa Faehndrich, Canadian Operational Support Command Headquarters, Ottawa; Chief Warrant Officer Gilda Dolph, Canadian Material Support Group, Ottawa; Master Warrant Officer Luanne MacKinney, 2 Air Movements Squadron, Trenton; Master Warrant Officer Colleen Halpin, 4 Canadian Forces Movement Control Unit, Montreal;

Warrant Officer Lisa Harvey, Transport and Rescue Standards and Evaluation Team, Trenton; and Sergeant Lucie Laporte, 2 Air Movements Squadron, Trenton.

Operational support capabilities such as aircraft ground-handling and air terminal services are vital to the efficient operation of CF transport aircraft. Each of the Canadian Air Force Wings maintains an Air Mobility Support terminal and qualified staff to provide that vital support to transient and integral aircraft at the Wing. In addition, four MAMS teams are based at 2 Air Movements Squadron, the CF's main air transport hub, at 8 Wing Trenton. These 12-person teams are kept at a high level of readiness to deploy anywhere in the world to perform a wide range of aircraft ground handling functions including freight preparation, cargo handling, aircraft loading/unloading and passenger processing for the CF, coalition and contracted aircraft. 2 Air Movements Squadron is thus credited with handling an average of 36 million pounds of freight and 42,000 passengers annually, both at home and abroad.

2 Air Movements Squadron and the smaller Air Mobility Support Sections at each of the Air Force Wings are established with personnel from the Traffic Tech (Non-Commissioned Member) and Logistics-Air (Officer) occupations. Air Mobility Support is a specific qualification within these professions that is given to those employed at the Wings and, for some, who are destined to become aircrew as loadmasters on the CC130 Hercules or CC150 Polaris aircraft.

The Traffic Tech trade as it is known today originated in 1945 when ground crews from 435 Squadron stationed in Burma expressed an interest in flying with the aerial delivery missions on the C-47 Dakota aircraft.[2] These first air movers or loadmasters were thus dubbed "kickers" because they assisted in kicking the loads out of the aircraft. These were dangerous combat missions that employed rudimentary aerial delivery techniques because the C-47 aircraft was equipped with only a single passenger door at one side of the aircraft.

From 1945 to 1952, the trade was formally named "Air Traffic Assistants" (ATA) and then later "Movement Controllers Air" (MCA). The MCA trade was populated with supply specialists from the Royal Canadian Ordnance Corps. Their work was physically demanding and rough. Aircraft loads were tied down to the cargo floor with half-inch manila rope (hemp or natural fibre), which would rip into the flesh on hands, arms and legs. Furthermore, many of the aircraft in this era did not have proper cargo doors or loading aids, requiring freight to be literally carried into the aircraft piece-by-piece.

In 1961, the introduction the CC130 Hercules and CC106 Yukon aircraft to the air transport fleet resulted in the considerable expansion of the occupation (now named "Transportation Technician") and the establishment of the Loadmaster position on the aircrews. By 1967, the first informal collection of MAMS personnel were assembled in Trenton by a rough-and-tumble group of technicians and were named the "Rogers Rangers" after the nominal leader of the group, Sergeant Bob Rogers. By the late 1960s, the increased frequency of deployed operations resulted in the establishment of three nine-person MAMS teams of which could be employed day-to-day at 2 Air Movements Unit in Trenton but could also rapidly deploy anywhere in the world.[3] Also during this era, with the formation of the Canadian Airborne Regiment, the tactical airlift role was developed. Aerial delivery capabilities were refined with the development of equipment rigging and parachute extraction procedures that required very specific qualifications for both Transportation Technicians and Loadmasters. By 1970, the former was renamed to "Traffic Technician."

Master Warrant Officer Luanne MacKinney
2 Air Movements Squadron, 8 Wing Trenton

Writing from the Transport Aircraft Unit (TAU) during the inaugural Operation Apollo mission in the Persian Gulf Region in 2002, in which the TAU was employed in both airlanded and tactical air transport (aerial delivery) missions over Iraq and Afghanistan:

Overall, the life of a female Traffic Tech is much the same as that of a male Traffic Tech. I have found that there is next to naught discrimination in regards to gender. I have heard my fellow male Traffic Techs say: 'If she can do the job, then that is fine by me,' to which I respond: 'If he can do the job, then that is fine by me.'

In 1976, the Traffic Tech trade was first opened to women, although at that time their employment was mostly limited to the administrative functions within the occupation, such as furniture and effects clerks, shipping and receiving clerks and passenger booking system operators. It would take more than ten years for the physically labour-intensive side of the trade on the line crews, MAMS teams and CC130 crews to become fully accessible to women. In 1985, a trial was conducted to determine if women had the sheer physical strength to be a crewmember on the Hercules, based on the upper-body strength required to access one of the overhead escape hatches that might be utilized in the event of ditching over water.[4] The trial was a success and by the next year, the first woman had qualified as an operational CC130 Loadmaster. Nearly thirty years after the trade was opened to women, it appointed its first female Chief Warrant Officer from within the Air Force ranks: Chief Warrant Officer Gilda Dolph subsequently took on her present duties at Canadian Material Support Group, Ottawa.[5] Approximately 20 years after the first woman qualified, women comprised approximately 6 percent of those traffic techs serving as loadmasters in the CF.[6]

Warrant Officer Lisa Harvey
CC130 Hercules Loadmaster
Transport and Rescue Standardization and Evaluation Team
8 Wing Trenton

Speaking at the 2006 *Women Leading in Defence* symposium, Kingston, Ontario:

When I started out in the Traffic Tech trade, my father said it would be a good choice if I wanted to travel. I thus identified being a Loadmaster as a career goal…but it took me 14 years to achieve it. After the birth of my first daughter, the powers-that-be assumed that I did not want to fly. Unbeknownst to me, my name was taken off the list of potential candidates for Loadmaster training. When I re-emphasized that I was still interested in Loadmaster employment, no opportunities were available. Finally, a year after the birth of my second daughter, I was selected to go flying.

Master Warrant Officer Colleen Halpin
4 Canadian Forces Movement Control Unit, Montreal

Speaking at the 2006 *Women Leading in Defence* symposium, Kingston, Ontario:

As a leader, I have always concentrated on being the best soldier, airman, or sailor, that I could be, and also being the best Traffic Technician that I can be, and tried to keep my gender out of it. I have always just concentrated on the job at hand…as a supervisor, manager and technician who "just happened" to also be a women. That has worked well, as I have gained the respect, although I may have lost something in not celebrating or acknowledging my diversity.

Master Warrant Officer Luanne MacKinney
2 Air Movements Squadron

Writing from the TAU during Operation Apollo MAMS operations on the ramp in the Persian Gulf Region in 2002:

We may have an extensive amount of dirt under our semi-manicured fingernails. Our combats may be dirty and torn from the concertina wire previously loaded on the Hercules. We may have vehicle hydraulic fluid smudged on our forehead and cheeks because we noticed a leak when doing the vehicle daily inspection on the K-25 loader. You may even not want to stand down wind of us because we are "glowing" with perspiration from a temperature that would fry an egg on the tarmac. Our boots may be scuffed and there may be strange and unusual things caught in our hair. But at the end of the shift, we are still women who appreciate a hot shower and our favorite shirt, jeans and shoes.

Traffic Techs, given the nature of their work that is often carried out under very austere and challenging conditions, have a reputation for being a burly, but down-to-earth bunch. They live by the age-old adage: "Work hard, play hard," and are proud of their sometimes unrefined demeanour. The Loadmasters have affectionately taken the pig as their mascot…for reasons that remain unclear…and operational Loadmasters with the prescribed number of flying hours are awarded the coveted pig coin. Women have nonetheless proudly thrived within the trade, and have persisted at challenging any barriers to their employment. In fact, today women are filling key roles on the flying squadrons and within the Air Mobility Support organizations across the CF.

Air Mobility Support personnel and air transport crews have deployed all over the world with increasing frequency, particularly since the late 1990s when the operational tempo of the CF as a whole skyrocketed. MAMS teams were sent out the door at such a pace that maintaining the line operations at 2 Air Movements Squadron and the Wings necessitated a wholesale reorganization of these resources accompanied by the development of a new system to manage the readiness and deployment of the teams.[7] The MAMS teams are very often the "first in and last out" of a theatre of operations, given that it is their job to receive and off-load the deployment aircraft. Employment at the Air Movements Squadron and deployment into a theatre of operations as part of a MAMS team is thus a great adventure, albeit very serious work in both combat and humanitarian operations.

Sergeant Lucie Laporte
2 Air Movements Squadron
8 Wing Trenton

During the first deployment of Operation Apollo in 2002 a skeleton crew was left to manage line operations at 8 Wing when three MAMS teams deployed to the Persian Gulf Region as part of the TAU. Writing from the rear party at 2 Air Movements Squadron, she says:

Our job may not be as high profile as pilots or doctors but the challenges and rewards are indescribable, especially after a job well done. We have the feeling that our work makes a real difference in someone's life when most needed. When a disaster or conflict occurs, we are among the first to deploy into a theatre of operations. During missions such as the floods in Manitoba [in 1997] and the earthquake in Turkey [in 1999], our teams were on the ground to distribute precious cargo such as construction materials, medical supplies and food.

Sergeant Laporte has recently returned from a six-month tour in Kabul, Afghanistan on Operation ARCHER.

Sergeant Lucie Laporte
2 Air Movements Squadron
8 Wing Trenton

She describes one of her experiences while employed on a line crew at 2 Air Movements Squadron and deployed on CC130 and CC150 missions as loadmaster:

On April 20, 2002, I was on a routine tasking in Germany, when our mission took a totally different turn. An accident near Kandahar had resulted in four Canadian casualties. Our aircraft, a CC150 Airbus, was tasked to bring the bodies home. Although emotionally a very difficult time, I listened carefully to instructions given by Loadmaster Sergeant Vickie Montag. The mission was carried out with the utmost respect and pride considering these tragic circumstances.[8]

MAMS teams have, for the most part, deployed in support of larger-scale missions, as is the case with the bulk of ongoing CF operations in Afghanistan and domestically for activities such as Operation BOXTOP, the semi-annual re-supply of Canada's northernmost outpost, Canadian Forces Station Alert. They have also deployed, however, as a stand-alone capability, as occurred in 1999 for Operation REPTILE in Sierra Leone. On that occasion, three MAMS teams deployed to the theatre of operations to ensure that the airport at Freetown remained open for the delivery of humanitarian aid to the region. MAMS teams have deployed with the Disaster Assistance Response Team (DART) on all of its operational deployments, including Operation CENTRAL (Hurricane Mitch, Honduras), Operation TORRENT (Earthquake, Turkey) and Operation STRUCTURE (Tsunami, Sri Lanka). On these occasions, as on many others, MAMS teams have deployed into austere and dangerous environments to carry out their duties with unsurpassed professionalism and commitment.

Warrant Officer Lisa Harvey
CC130 Hercules Loadmaster
Transport and Rescue Standardization and Evaluation Team
8 Wing Trenton

Speaking at the 2006 *Women Leading in Defence* symposium, Kingston, Ontario:

I do feel a constant need to be just as good as the guys, because I do not want them to feel that I am not pulling my end of the workload. On my Basic Tactical Air Transport course, after we completed an aerial delivery of paratroopers, I attempted to close the paratrooper door on the side of the aircraft. No matter how hard I tried, it would not close. My instructor, who was standing behind me, offered to help. I refused his help and continued to try and close the door on my own. Finally, exhausted, I gave up. The instructor, a fairly big strong lad, took over, but he could not close the door either. I was so relieved! I was so scared he was going to think he had to close the door for the girl. As it turned out, the angle of the airframe was creating too much wind resistance at the door, which had to be corrected before it could be closed.

The integration of women into the Traffic Tech trade, originally established in the 1940s, has had a relatively short history of twenty-six years. Many of their male counterparts at the higher ranks within the trade began their careers when women were restricted from the more physically demanding functions of the trade, which has had an impact on the success of this integration – something that continues to be felt, even today. Nonetheless, the women who have excelled as Traffic Techs in both the Air Force and Army environments have pulled their weight while fitting into the "work hard, play hard" mantra. These women, and men, have switched seamlessly between employment on Land Forces Command Bases and as line crew or Loadmasters on the Air Force Wings. They have worked in joint environments supporting CF Operations in Units such as 4 Canadian Forces Movement Control Unit and as integral members of missions all over the world. They have struggled with balancing a career and family, prioritizing the careers of married service couples, and all of the challenges that we face as members of the CF. As members of a support trade, and as women in a support trade, they have perhaps not been adequately recognized for these efforts over the years...nor do they want to be...

ENDNOTES

1   Effective January 1, 2007. Data provided by Director Human Rights and Diversity, National Defence Headquarters, Ottawa.

2   Data gleaned from the Logistics Movers Association web-site (www.lmacanada.ca) and the Logistics Branch Secretariat web-site (http://www.forces.gc.ca/admmat/logbranch/index_e.asp).

3   Pickett, J. & A. Caza, "2 Air Movements Squadron 50th Anniversary," *Logistics Branch Bulletin* Vol. 2, Issue 3, October 2001.

4   Then Capt C.M. Faehndrich of 5 Air Movements Unit, Lahr was chosen to be the test candidate on the CC130 Hercules Loadmaster Course in 1985.

5   Traffic Technicians are divided in assignment between both the Air Force and Army elements; however, the uniform that they are assigned does not restrict their employment. Both Air Force and Army Traffic Technicians are employed in their assigned roles across all three elements, regardless of the uniform that they wear.

6   At time of writing, 99 of 535 traffic technicians were serving as loadmasters, six women and 93 men. Chief Warrant Officer J.A.J. Boisvert, Traffic Technician Career Manager, Director Military Careers. Personal Communication (March 15, 2007).

7   This reorganization resulted in the closure of 1 Air Movements Squadron in Winnipeg in 2006. Personnel and resources from this unit were reallocated to 2 Air Movements Squadron and Wings such as 4 Wing Cold Lake and 19 Wing Comox.

8   On April 17, 2002 , Sergeant Marc Léger, Corporal Ainsworth Dyer, Private Nathan Smith, and Private Richard Green, died as a result of 'friendly fire' – a bomb dropped from a United States F-16 aircraft on a section of the Princess Patricia's Canadian Light Infantry (PPCLI) during a training exercise that they were participating in at Tarnak Farm outside of Kandahar, Afghanistan. See, for example, Michael Friscolanti, *Friendly Fire: The Untold Story of the U.S. Bombing That Killed Four Canadian Soldiers in Afghanistan*. (Mississauga: John Wiley & Sons Canada, Ltd., 2005).

CHAPTER 7

From Ocean Ops to Combat Ops: A Short History of Women and Leadership in the Canadian Forces

Lieutenant-Commander (retired) Karen D. Davis

The experience of an Oceanographic Operator (Ocean Op) in the Canadian Forces (CF) 25 or 30 years ago provides a significant contrast to the experience of a woman serving in the combat arms in 2007. It is obvious that gender integration has come a long way, and this progress clearly reflects the ability of women to make significant contributions to the CF. The increased participation of women in the CF also represents Canadian values reflected by legislation and the persistent efforts of many in ensuring that women are afforded equitable opportunity to participate in the defence of Canada. At every step of the journey, the integration of women, now referred to as gender integration, has met some resistance ranging from skepticism in reference to the ability of women to do the job to social resistance to the very idea of women in the military, and ultimately women in combat roles. Beginning with a brief look at my experience as an ocean op, this chapter discusses some of the key milestones along the way, thus highlighting the efforts that have been necessary to ensure gender integration continued to move forward over the past several decades.

In 1978, I joined the CF as an Oceanographic Operator (Ocean Op), the only *all female* occupation in the CF at the time. The rationale provided for an all female occupation made reference to the unique abilities of women in terms of manual dexterity and paying close attention to detail. In fact, the strategy for employing only women as ocean ops was similar, if not the same, as the strategy used to employ women in the Women's Royal Canadian Naval Service (WRCNS), the Canadian Women's Army Corps (CWAC), and the

Royal Canadian Air Force Women's Division (RCAF WD) during World War II – to free men for war, and in peacetime for deployed operational positions. Women, including Ocean Ops, were restricted from sea duty in 1978, and thus provided a female workforce to conduct underwater acoustic analysis in shore stations so that the sonarmen, who were also acoustic analysts, were free to serve at sea.

As an Ocean Op, I joined a female naval community. The first Ocean Ops, many still serving when I joined, had started out as radar plotters. With the technological developments of the Cold War, female radar plotters were reassigned as the first members of the new ocean op trade. As the ocean op trade was becoming established, sonarmen shared their analytical experience in several of the operational supervisory roles[1]; however by 1978 when I joined, the Ocean Ops had developed a core of technical expertise and were capable of operating quite independently. As a result, all of the supervisors and senior non-commissioned leaders to whom I reported, were women. It was normal for me to work for female Chief Petty Officers and Petty Officers who were in senior leadership positions as Ocean Ops. All of the officers were male maritime surface and sub-surface (MARS) officers as women were not permitted in the MARS occupation at the time. The exceptions were female Reserve Force junior officers who were occasionally assigned to Canadian Forces Station (CFS) Shelburne, Nova Scotia as watch officers.

All of the equipment and communications technicians at the shore station were men in male only occupations at the time – sailors on 'shore postings'. The Ocean Ops were the operational shift workers covering 24 hours a day, seven days a week, while many of those who were not Ocean Ops, worked Monday to Friday as 'day workers'. As a result the female Ocean Ops were the operators that were responsible for a variety of emergency situations, including firefighting, should it be required. There was a three-week naval firefighting course that was held in Halifax at the time, but in the early 1980s women were still not eligible to attend this course. Regardless of the fact that we did not have access to the same standard of training as our male peers, firefighting, including the leadership and coordination of the on-site firefighting efforts, remained our responsibility. Definitely there were some challenges, but as young women in the CF, we faced them together. We did question policies such as those that excluded us from required training, but from our perspective, no one was really listening and we just carried on.

In lieu of the three-week firefighting course, the Ocean Ops did receive a short course that was locally designed and delivered by the civilian firemen on the station. As a junior supervisor in 1981, I was attending one of these local courses with the other members of my operational section. As the ultimate 'test' of our firefighting skills, we were outfitted in firefighting clothing and chemical oxygen equipment, and sent into an old World War II bunker to put out a fire that had been set by the instructors. One of the Ocean Ops on my section was quite fearful and reluctant to enter the burning bunker, so the instructors encouraged her to select a student or instructor of her choice as her firefighting partner to increase her confidence. We all assumed that she would choose one of the male instructors or one of the two sailors who were assisting with the course, and who had previously completed the three-week navy firefighting course. Much to my surprise she chose me. My initial reaction was fear that I would somehow let her down, as she seemed to have so much confidence in my ability to lead her through a potentially dangerous task. I have always remembered this incident as one of the turning points in my understanding of the responsibilities of leadership. We did extinguish that fire without incident!

Upon promotion to Leading Wren[2] in 1982, my direct supervisor, a Petty Officer 1st Class, presented me with my own copy of the navy *Divisional System*, along with her guidance to me on the importance of my responsibilities as a leader. As a Leading Wren, I took that responsibility seriously and did my utmost to meet what I perceived as the expectations for me to effectively teach and coach subordinates, lead by example, and focus on continued excellence in applying and developing my trade knowledge. Indeed, the leadership example that was set by senior Ocean Ops was one of professionalism, discipline, personal integrity, a high level of technical expertise, and pride in their uniform and contribution to naval operations.

My first experiences in male dominated situations were in the context of general training. In 1980, on a Unit Physical Training Assistant (UPTA) Course at Canadian Forces Base Borden, I was exposed for the first time to a male-dominated environment as one of two women on a course of 15 students (most from the Canadian Airborne Regiment and 2 Princess Patricia Canadian Light Infantry) and all male course instructors. For me, a physically demanding course, but I met the challenge with the full support of most of my peers and instructors. In 1983, on my Junior Leader Course (JLC) in Halifax, I was one of three women on a course of 61 students, almost all from the sea environment. On each of these courses, I was treated with respect by enough of my peers and instructors to result in very positive and professional learning experiences. Indeed, throughout the rest of my time in uniform, as a junior Non-Commissioned Member (NCM) and officer, I looked back to my JLC, as the best leadership training I had ever received.

In 1985, the all-female tradition was ended when the first male became an Ocean Op. Rationale for segregated male and female employment based upon such attributes as manual dexterity and attention to detail were abandoned. Upon completion of initial trade training, the first qualified male Ocean Op was posted to the Canadian Forces detachment at the United States Naval Station Argentia, Newfoundland. In Argentia, Canadian Ocean Ops worked alongside United States Navy Oceansystems Technicians (OTs), who were male and female. About the same time, I was promoted to Master Seaman, posted to Argentia, and as an on-watch supervisor, I assumed responsibility for the direct supervision of the Canadian male Ocean Op along with several male OTs. This was my first experience supervising men, but the greatest challenges I faced in Argentia were related to negotiating the subtle differences in the Canadian and U.S. naval cultures.

By 1983, I was beginning to question why women could not serve at sea, and was frequently incensed by the derogatory comments that were rumoured around the navy about Ocean Ops – that they were either promiscuous or lesbian. In fact, I was still posted to CFS Shelburne, Nova Scotia in 1983 when investigations of women suspected of being lesbian were underway. In my experience, the investigations and subsequent accusations were extremely effective in destroying the morale and overall operational effectiveness of a military unit. Unfortunately, it would take another ten years to lift the restrictions on the employment of homosexuals in the CF.[3] It was not until I attended university years later that I began to gain a broader understanding of the social and historical processes that influence the persistent labeling of women's sexuality and social behaviour in male dominated cultures. I believe that such understanding is an important aspect of professional development and success for women in masculine cultures such as the CF.

Overall, my knowledge of organizational and social processes at the time of the Shelburne investigations was limited to my immediate situation, and it all seemed incredibly cruel and unfair. Indeed, I had little awareness of the social forces that were shaping the experience of women in Canada, including the CF response that was influencing access to equitable opportunities for women in the CF. The discussion below provides some of the highlights of the contemporary social and legal processes in Canada and CF responses that have influenced the current status of women in the CF today.

The Royal Commission on the Status of Women: 1969

The report of the Royal Commission on the Status of Women, published in 1970, marked a turning point for women in Canadian society, including women in the Canadian military. The commission made 167 recommendations for changes considered necessary to provide a climate of equal opportunity for women in Canada and six of these pertained to women in the Canadian Forces. Specifically, the commission sought:

- standardization of enrolment criteria;

- equal pension benefits for women and men;

- the opportunity for women to attend Canadian Military Colleges;

- the opening of all trades and officer classifications to women; and

- the termination of regulations which prohibited the enrolment of married women and required the release of servicewomen on the birth of a child.[4]

By 1971, married women could join the CF, women who gave birth to a child could continue to serve, women were eligible for subsidized education at civilian universities as officer candidates in the Regular Officer Training Plan (ROTP), and women became eligible to serve in a broader range of roles. However, they were still excluded from serving in primary combat roles, in remote locations, and at sea,[5] and attending military college.

Since 1971, officer classifications and NCM trades had been open to women in engineering, dental, air traffic, air weapons, legal, logistics, security, and air technician fields.[6] By 1974, there were well over 2,000 women in the CF employed in 33 of 95 trades, comprising approximately three percent of the Regular Force. In 1975, amendments were made to the Canadian Forces Superannuation Act to make pension contributions and benefits the same for women and men.[7] By 1978, 4,786 women comprised 5.9 percent of the CF Regular Force[8] and were eligible to serve in 81 of 127 officer and NCM occupations.[9]

Canadian Human Rights Act: 1978

Over the next years and decades the CF faced numerous legal challenges and questioned the utility of women's employment in the military from numerous angles. As a result of the proclamation of the Canadian Human Rights Act in 1978, the Canadian Forces could limit the employment of women, only if they could base that restriction on *bona fide* requirements; that is, by demonstrating that women could not perform the job "safely, efficiently and reliably".[10] In June 1978, and in anticipation of the impending impact of the Canadian Human Rights Act on the CF, the CF Directorate of Personnel Development Studies published the findings of a survey in reference to the employment of women in combat roles and isolated postings, which had been administered to over 4,000 CF members and their spouses.[11] The majority of those polled expressed support for providing women with the opportunity to serve as aircrew, most of those polled were opposed to women serving in the combat arms and in submarines, and opinion was split in reference to women serving onboard naval destroyers. With the exception of spouses, most respondents believed that women should have the opportunity to serve at isolated postings. For the most part, opinion was directly related to

Photo courtesy of Major Anne Reiffenstein

Major Anne Reiffenstein (right), Battalion Commander, A Battery, 1 Royal Canadian Horse Artillery (1RCHA) debriefing Lieutenant Nichola Goddard, Gun Position Officer, on the conduct of an open action shoot. October 2003

Photo courtesy of Major Anne Reiffenstein

Lieutenant Nichola Goddard, Platoon Commander, A Battery, 1 Royal Canadian Horse Artillery (1RCHA), on Operation PEREGRINE after fighting fires in the mountain areas of Chase, British Columbia. August 2003

Photo courtesy of Major Anne Reiffenstein

Lieutenant Nichola Goddard (left) in a reconnaissance Armoured Personnel Carrier (APC) on exercise. 2003

Photo: Master Corporal Paul MacGregor, Canadian Forces Combat Camera

AMPARA, SRI LANKA
Major Steve Hewitt, Company Commander with the Canadian Forces Disaster Assistance Response Team (DART), discusses possible problems with fellow team members Captain Suzan Seo and Captain Lena Cormier. January 2005

Photo: Master Corporal Paul MacGregor, Canadian Forces Combat Camera

AMPARA, SRI LANKA
Captain Sarah Heer, a member of the Canadian Forces Disaster Assistance Response Team (DART), marks a grid on the map during a humanitarian assistance operation.
January 2005

Photo: Sergeant Frank Hudec, Canadian Forces Combat Camera

GARHI DOPATTA, PAKISTAN
Major Julia Atherley-Blight, Deputy Commanding Officer of the Canadian Forces Disaster Assistance Response Team (DART), salutes during a Remembrance Day ceremony while deployed on Operation PLATEAU, an earthquake relief effort. November 2005

Photo: Corporal David Cribb

CANADIAN FORCES BASE TRENTON, ONTARIO
Major Annette Snow, Flight Surgeon and Chief Medical Officer for the Canadian Disaster Relief Team preparing to depart to flood-stricken New Orleans, speaks with the media on the role of Canadian Forces and her team. September 2005

Photo courtesy of Captain J.J. Longley

AFGHANISTAN
Captain Jodi-Jane Longley of 436 Transport Squadron Trenton monitoring fuel panels on a CC130 Hercules aircraft during a fuel re-supply mission. 2006

Photo: Master Corporal Paul MacGregor, Canadian Forces Combat Camera

WAINWRIGHT, ALBERTA
Corporal Bill Deschamp (left) and Private Shelly Munro, both Aviation Technicians (AVN Tech) with 408 Tactical Helicopter Squadron (Edmonton), reinstall an engine component on a CH-146 Griffon helicopter during Exercise RESOLUTE WARRIOR. April 2003

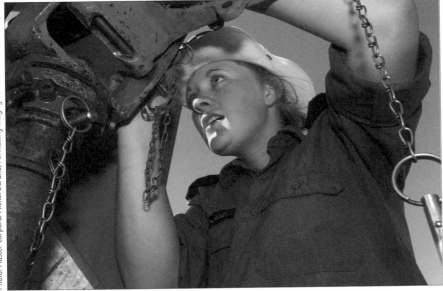

Photo: Master Corporal Michel Durand, Formatting Imaging Services Halifax

HER MAJESTY'S CANADIAN SHIP (HMCS), ST. JOHN'S
Ordinary Seaman Janna Strickland, a Boatswain (Bosn), prepares her 50 calibre machine-gun prior to a boarding exercise during Operation APOLLO, Canada's military contribution to the international campaign against terrorism. May 2002

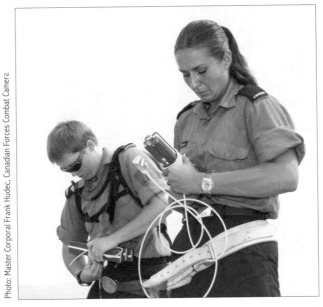

Photo: Master Corporal Frank Hudec, Canadian Forces Combat Camera

HER MAJESTY'S CANADIAN SHIP (HMCS) REGINA, GULF OF OMAN, ARABIAN GULF REGION
Leading Seaman Mandy Dagenais and Ordinary Seaman Kris Correa prepare demolition charges to destroy a simulated mine during Pouncer Operations in the Gulf of Oman. April 2003

HER MAJESTY'S CANADIAN SHIP (HMCS) OTTAWA, ARABIAN GULF
Naval boarding party member Leading Seaman Catherine Gabanna, fires her 9mm Sig Sauer pistol while conducting live fire training on the flight deck during Operation ENDURING FREEDOM. November 2006

Photo: Sergeant Dennis Mah, Canadian Forces Combat Camera

BOSNIA-HERZEGOVINA
Quick Reaction Force member, Reservist Corporal Helen Pagistakis (front) runs for cover as other members of her team take up positions to defend the Griffon helicopter that delivered them to this hilltop exercise area during Operation PALLADIUM, Canada's contribution to the NATO Stabilization Force (SFOR). June 2001

Photo: Master Corporal Jeff D. de Molitor

ARABIAN GULF REGION

Master Corporal Janine Henderson, an Avionics Tech from 8 Wing Trenton, Ontario, walks out to the front of a CC130 Hercules aircraft after giving it a final check before it takes off with a load of supplies destined for Kandahar, Afghanistan in support of Operation APOLLO. March 2002

Photo courtesy of: Corporal Kim Gosse

Master Warrant Officer Gilda Dolph of 2 Air Movements, 8 Wing Trenton supervises CC130 Hercules loading operations. August 2002

Photo: Sergeant Gerry Pilote, Canadian Forces Combat Camera

VELIKA KLADUSA, BOSNIA
Flight engineer Warrant Officer Lyne Deshaies operates the C6 light machine-gun mounted in the side door of a CH-146 Griffon flown by 430 Tactical Helicopter Squadron from Valcartier. November 2001

Photo: Master Corporal Paul MacGregor, Canadian Forces Combat Camera

ZGON, BOSNIA-HERZEGOVINA
Corporal Amber Churchill, a member of the Lord Strathcona's Horse (LdSH) "B" Squadron, chats with grade eight children during a school visit in the city of Sanski Most, Bosnia-Herzegovina. November 2002

Photo: Corporal John Bradley, 3 Royal 22ᵉ Régiment Battalion Group

KABUL, AFGHANISTAN
Corporal Michelle Tremblay from the National Support Element (NSE) Transport Platoon, Task Force Kabul, Operation ATHENA, stands in the driver's hatch of her Bison armoured vehicle. July 2004

Photo: Sergeant Frank Hudec, Canadian Forces Combat Camera

KABUL, AFGHANISTAN
Lieutenant Kathy Hanna, a troop commmander with 2 Royal Canadian Horse Artillery (2RCHA), unloads a Browning 9mm semi-automatic pistol into a clearing bay at the Canadian International Security Assistance Force (ISAF) camp in Kabul, Afghanistan during Operation ATHENA. August 2003

Photo: Corporal Doug Farmer

KABUL, AFGHANISTAN
Bombardier Marie Robert, serving with the Unmanned Aerial Vehicle (UAV) Troop of 2 Royal Canadian Horse Artillery Regiment (2RCHA), guides the Sperwer UAV as it is hoisted onto the catapult ramp prior to launch during Operation ATHENA. November 2003

Photo: Master Corporal Robert Bottrill, Canadian Forces Combat Camera

KANDAHAR AIR FIELD, AFGHANISTAN
Corporal Kristie McKay with Task Force Afghanistan, places her poppy in a wreath following the conclusion of the Remembrance Day ceremony. November 2005

Photo: Canadian Forces Combat Camera

ZEBALLOS, VANCOUVER ISLAND, BRITISH COLUMBIA
Chuck Syme, 4th Canadian Ranger Patrol Group, and Private Leona M.A. Chaisson, an Imagery Technician with Canadian Forces Base Esquimalt, en route to a Canadian Ranger exercise on Nootka Island, British Columbia. July 2006

Photo: Corporal Bill Gomm, 38 Combat Brigade

WINNIPEG, MANITOBA
Private Priska Zinn, 6 Intelligence Company, 38 Canadian Brigade plots contact information on the map during Exercise THINKING BISON. March 2006

Photo: Corporal Charles Barber, Canadian Forces Base Esquimalt Imaging Services

PACIFIC COAST, NORTH AMERICA
Ordinary Seaman Jennifer Courneyea (left), a naval communicator aboard the Canadian replenishment ship Her Majesty's Canadian Ship (HMCS) Protecteur, uses flags (semaphore) to pass a message to the frigate HMCS Regina during a replenishment-at-sea (RAS) to receive fuel. December 2003

respondent perceptions of the impact that women would have on operational effectiveness. For example, most opposed the service of women in the combat arms and most perceived that operational effectiveness would be degraded if women were introduced into the combat arms. On the other hand, a majority supported the service of women on support ships and most believed that the presence of women would neither impact nor improve, the operational effectiveness of support ships.

Overall, serving women were the most optimistic of those surveyed and most indicated that they would be willing to serve in most of the roles in question. Those issues perceived to present the most serious challenges to the employment of women in non-traditional roles, included women's physical capabilities, marital conflict, the emotional suitability of women, and the impact of women on operational effectiveness.[12]

In addition to the CF survey, Gallup Canada conducted opinion polls in November 1977 and May 1978 on behalf of the Department of National Defence, regarding the employment of women in active military combat roles. Overall, the responses indicated that more Canadians supported the service of women in all roles than were against the idea in any particular role. Support for women as aircrew was clearly the strongest, while support for women in land combat units was the weakest. Also, a smaller proportion of females than of males were in favour of female employment in combat roles.[13] This research laid the groundwork for the Servicewomen in Non-Traditional Environments and Roles (SWINTER) trials.

Servicewomen in Non-Traditional Environments and Roles: 1979-1985

Socio-demographic and legal considerations were cited as the rationale for the CF to re-examine policies in reference to the employment of women.[14] The SWINTER trials, conducted from 1979-1985, were designed to assist the CF in assessing the impact of women's employment on the operational effectiveness of previously all-male units. Specifically, the following considerations formed the basis of the SWINTER trials:

- the effectiveness of individual servicewomen versus servicemen for representative work at trial units;

- the effectiveness of groups of servicewomen, similar groups of servicemen, and integrated groups of women and men when conducting representative work at trial units;

- the behavioural and sociological impact of servicewomen on trial units, including the sociological impact on the immediate families of personnel at trial units;

- the degree of acceptance of the public and our allies for the employment of servicewomen in non-traditional roles and environments; and

- the resource implications of the expanded participation of servicewomen in the CF.[15]

The trial research included participant observation at previously all-male units, and questionnaire administration to women and men serving in the SWINTER trial units. The SWINTER trial units included field service support to primary land combat operations (4 Service Battalion and 4 Field Ambulance), service at sea in a support capacity aboard a non-combatant ship (HMCS *Cormorant*), support to operations at an isolated communications station located above the Arctic Circle (CFS Alert), and as aircrew at transport (436 Squadron) or transport and search-and-rescue squadrons (413, 424, 435, and 442 Squadron). To conduct the trials, servicewomen were assigned to such units on a trial basis in roles that had previously excluded women.[16]

The SWINTER trials produced strong evidence to show that factors other than the actual abilities and performance of servicewomen influenced male attitudes toward women and ultimately the extent of integration achieved.[17] Consequently, the SWINTER research concluded that the "adoption of a 'business as usual' approach" would not provide sufficient guidance in creating positive integration of women into previously all-male domains. That is, effective integration would be dependent upon leadership in addressing real and perceived issues such as compromised selection and training standards, harassment of women, resistance to change, restrictions in range of tasks that supervisors assign women, differences in the physical strength and aggressiveness of women and men, women's fearfulness, emotionality and pregnancy, sexual relationships between men and women who are working together, and rumours of women's homosexuality.[18,19] Although women were not assigned combat duties in the SWINTER trials, the trials did provide an opportunity for further policy development and a re-thinking of the ways in which the CF could or should be responsive to changes in social practice and attitudes during the 1980s.[20] In this sense, the stage was set for subsequent expansion of the roles and employment of women in the CF.

In 1986, the CF announced that women would be eligible to serve in mixed-gender occupations within seven classes of units within the Regular Force which were previously designated male only: Auxiliary Oil Replenishment Ships; Service Battalions; Field Ambulance Units; Maritime Patrol Squadrons; Maritime Reconnaissance Squadrons; Electronic Warfare Squadrons (Air); and Military Police Platoons. In addition, two previously male-only military occupations were opened to the participation of women: Airborne Electronic Sensor Operator; and, Preventative Medicine Technician.[21]

Combat Related Employment of Women: 1987

Subsequent to the 1985 Parliamentary Committee on Equality Rights, a 1986 CF Charter Task Force on Equality Issues recommended further expansion of the roles of women in the CF. In addition, the task force recommended the development of a program to provide detailed policy guidance and leadership training concerning mixed-gender employment.[22] In 1987, the Minister of National Defence tasked the Department of National Defence with various initiatives related to expanding the employment of women in the CF, including intensified recruiting programs targeting potential female recruits,[23] and the development of trial options with remaining male-only units and occupations.[24] Combat Related Employment of Women (CREW) trials were designed for the Army and Navy to evaluate mixed- and single-gender combat units and ships to determine if there would be any reduction in operational effectiveness due to the introduction of women.[25] A CREW trial plan was not developed for the Air Force as there were no formally stated limitations to the employment of women, even though women had not yet been employed in several air units and occupations at that time.

Canadian Human Rights Tribunal: 1989

From 1986 to 1988, the Canadian Human Rights Tribunal sat to hear four separate but related complaints, regarding opportunities for training and employment in the CF. The complaints, submitted to the Canadian Human Rights Commission, in 1981, 1982, 1983 and 1984, concerned: the denial of a transfer of a female administrative clerk to a regiment that had a 10 percent quota for women; the exclusion of women from risks assumed by men by prohibiting women from flying fighter aircraft; denial of training and employment opportunities for a female as a marine engineering technician; and denial of an employment opportunity for a trained female mechanic in a tactical helicopter squadron.[26] In the latter case, a settlement was reached before the final Tribunal decision, with the CF acknowledging that the refusal to employ the complainant in a helicopter squadron was due to an administrative error. In response to the remaining cases, the CF did not deny that its existing policies and practices were discriminatory, but contended that they were based upon *bona fide* occupational requirements, which the organization interpreted as 'operational effectiveness'. The Tribunal decision resulted in direction to the CF to proceed with the full integration of women into all roles and occupations in the following 10-year period. The tribunal directed that the conduct of the CREW trials proposed by the CF in 1987 would continue, but were not to be regarded as 'trials'. The CREW trials were to serve as the lead-up or preparation for full integration of women into all CF occupations and roles.[27]

Prompted by both the decision of the 1989 Canadian Human Rights Tribunal Ruling and to some extent the pending application of the Employment Equity Act[28] to the CF, the 1990s were by far the most active years in terms of research and activity to facilitate the increased participation of women in the military. Immediately following the Canadian Human Rights Tribunal direction, formal restrictions on the employment of women in the CF were removed, opening the door for women to participate in all roles and occupations with the exception of submarines and as ordained Roman Catholic chaplains.[29] In February 1990, the Minister of National Defence established a Minister's Advisory Board on Women in the Canadian Forces (MABWCF), later changed to the Minister's Advisory Board on Gender Integration in the Canadian Forces (MABGICF), to ensure compliance with the Tribunal direction and to facilitate external monitoring of the integration of women.[30] While the CF addressed many of the recommendations presented in the first four annual reports of the board, by 1995 and its fifth report the board believed that "…research, leadership and action in basic areas of personnel management and operations…" remained outstanding.[31]

With the exception of the monitoring conducted by the MABWCF/MABGICF, research in the early 1990s was focused primarily on quantitative monitoring of the status of women and psychometric analyses of CF selection tests. Analysis during this period did reveal test bias disadvantaging women on both officer and non-commissioned member selection tests. As a result, new tests have been developed and validation research is continuously conducted to ensure that the CF is not using selection tools that introduce gender bias.[32] Analysis was also conducted on the attrition of women and men from the CF,[33] the family status of women in the CF,[34] the career progression of women in the CF,[35] the status of trained women in the CF,[36] and the impact of downsizing of the CF on women.[37] This research was significant in that it informed the CF of the issues that were impacting the participation of women. Research designed to explore and measure the experiences of women in the CF was also introduced in the early 1990s. A qualitative study based on in-depth interviews with women who had left the CF, provided an initial exploratory look at experiences underlying different attrition rates among women and men. It concluded that family obligations and issues related to harassment and discrimination were influencing the attrition of women from the CF.[38]

Throughout the 1990s, the CF also placed considerable focus on harassment. A baseline harassment survey was administered to CF personnel in 1992,[39] followed by a replication survey in 1998.[40] These surveys informed the development of CF harassment policy and gender integration processes as the results confirmed that women were more likely than men to experience all types of harassment measured (sexual, personal and abuse of authority). In 1992, of those surveyed in the CF Regular Force, 26.2 percent of women and 2 percent of the men believed that they had experienced sexual harassment; 32.6 percent of women and 19.4 percent of men reported experience of personal harassment; and 31.5 percent of women and 28.9 percent of men reported experience of abuse of authority. Reported rates of harassment in the 1998 survey were down from 1992, with the exception of sexual harassment among male respondents which increased from 2 to 3 percent.[41] The Reserve Force was also surveyed in 1998. Overall, the reported rates of harassment were lower than among Regular Force members; however, like the Regular Force, women were more likely to report experience of harassment than men.[42]

In 1997, research was conducted to determine why the attrition of women from the combat arms was five times greater than the departure rate of men from the combat arms. Focus groups were conducted with serving women and men in the combat arms occupations and combat service support units,[43] and in-depth interviews were conducted with women who had left the combat arms.[44] This work focused on the experience of women and men in the CF training and employment environment as well as the experience of women who had served in the combat arms between 1989 and 1997. The research concluded that women faced significant social and psychological barriers. Overall, women were confronted by pre-conceived perceptions of their ability and motivation, informed by masculine cultural assumptions about gender roles and the social and sexual behaviour of women who choose traditional male employment.[45]

The mid-1990s and the 1995 employment equity legislation further prompted the CF to broaden equity and human rights research. In 1995, a survey was administered to CF members to gather attitudinal information regarding diversity.[46] However, this survey did not provide any information that could be linked to issues impacting gender integration. Consequently, the CF developed a Mixed Gender Opinion Questionnaire in 1997,[47] which was subsequently included as a scale in a re-administration of the diversity survey in 1999.[48]

By the end of the late 1990s, the focus of most human rights and equity research had shifted to employment equity and diversity as the CF worked to satisfy the requirements of the 1995 Employment Equity Act. In partial fulfillment of this objective, DND sanctioned and subsequently funded advisory groups representing each of the four employment equity designated groups: Advisory Group for Persons With Disabilities; Defence Aboriginal Advisory Group; Defence Visible Minority Advisory Group; and the Defence Women's Advisory Organization. All groups were stood up by 2000 and have since expended significant effort and resources on providing subject matter expertise and analytical input into various policy, program and organizational issues determined to have a potential impact on individuals represented by the groups. There are potential implications for women across all designated groups, and women are represented most broadly across the CF, relative to the members of other designated groups. As a result, the range of perspectives and experiences that the Defence Women's Advisory Organization must strive to represent are daunting, not to mention instructive of the need for both focused and integrated approaches to including the knowledge, perspective and experiences of women in future developments in the CF.

As the 1999 10-year milestone of the Canadian Human Rights Tribunal approached, activity shifted from research to action around program and planning to demonstrate progress and commitment to the Canadian Human Rights Commission (CHRC). The environmental commands shared this responsibility, with each presenting a plan for gender integration to the CHRC prior to the 1999 decision on CF progress. In addition, the Chief of the Maritime Staff released a research report that concluded that there was no sufficient reason to continue to exclude women from submarine service.[49] This research provided substantial input into the subsequent removal of restrictions preventing women from submarine service in the CF, thus removing the last formal CF barrier to the full participation of women.[50] In the final analysis, the CHRC was not satisfied with the progress that the CF had made in the last ten years; however, it was satisfied that senior leadership was sufficiently committed to gender integration in the future.

Into the 21st Century

Since 1999, relatively little research has been conducted on issues impacting women or gender integration in the CF. The Employment Equity Act places emphasis on the reporting of representative numbers within each of four designated groups: women, Aboriginal people, visible minorities and persons with disabilities. Women overall are represented in higher numbers than the other designated groups and are represented in most occupations and roles. This relative status of integration when compared to the other designated groups reinforces the perspective that women are fully integrated within the CF. In addition, general acceptance of widely promoted popular literature on changing values in society[51] has reinforced an understanding that male or female, you are impacted by the same issues with little recognition of the inequitable impact and outcome or the continuing disproportionate impact of some issues on women. For example, although the participation of men in family and household roles has increased, women continue to have disproportionate responsibility for the well-being of children and family.

Regardless, women are finding their place in the CF in increasing roles and domains, including senior leadership positions. Today, over 8,000 women are serving in the Regular Force Component, and an additional 15,000 serve in the Reserves on full and part-time commitments. Overall, representation is 13.2 percent and 20.5 percent in the Regular and Reserve Forces, respectively.[52] The representation of women in the Regular Force ranges from approximately 72 percent in the nursing occupation and 78 percent of dental hygienists to less than four percent of naval maintenance, electrical, mechanical, and military engineering trades, pilots, and soldiers and officers in the land combat arms.[53] There are over 450 women in the Regular Force senior officer corps[54] comprising approximately 9.6 percent of senior officers, and over 350 women in the Reserve Force senior officer corps comprising 7.7 percent of senior officers.[55] There are 1,250 women serving in the Regular Force and 1,590 in the Reserve Force as senior NCMs[56], representing approximately 9.6 and 12.8 percent, respectively, of the senior non-commissioned ranks.[57] As leadership at these senior rank levels has a significant impact on the implementation of policy, and the culture of the military, there is no doubt that women are leading and making substantial contributions to the CF.

The representation of women in leadership roles, and in operational leadership roles in particular, remains quite low. However, there are increasing numbers of women participating in combat and combat service support leadership roles in operational environments. Such change is progress, but it also presents significant challenges for women in terms of being able to identify with the women leaders who preceded them. How does a woman find her place and her pride in a tradition to which women have no history?[58] The women who joined the combat arms in the early 1990s were, for the most part, completely on their own in terms of finding their place in the regiment. Success meant that from the very beginning they had to possess many of the qualities of a good leader to survive because there was no one there to show them the way. Today, some of the women entering the combat arms are fortunate enough to be following in the footsteps of other successful women. Maybe with less pressure to feel responsible for demonstrating that women can do the job and deserve the opportunity to try, more energy can be focused on training and development.

Thirty years ago, Ocean Ops had many of those things that women in the combat arms do not have today. Ocean Ops had a defined place in the organization, they had women leaders and role models, and they had the utmost confidence of many that they had the technical abilities required for the job. When I went on the UPTA course in 1980 and my JLC in 1983, I encountered very little resistance from peers or leaders. For those short periods of four and five weeks of training I was able to integrate into the training environment with relative ease, and with the full knowledge that upon completion I would return to my job as an Ocean Op. However, opportunities for Ocean Ops were contained within a narrow domain that defined the limits of possibility, influenced, for example, by assumptions that women could not and should not serve at sea. Concurrent with other gender integration initiatives, such restrictions were slowly removed and Ocean Ops were provided with limited opportunities to serve at sea. For example, I was one of the first two Ocean Ops to serve for two weeks at sea as part of a naval exercise in the Pacific in 1985. Some Ocean Ops served at sea with the U.S. Navy long before the trade was rolled into Towed Array Surveillance operator (TAS Op) in the early 1990s and male and female TAS Ops served on board Canadian ships.[59] In this sense, the women who were Radar Plotters, then Ocean Ops, and then TAS Ops, have been incrementally integrated to become full participants and contributors to the evolution and change that has taken place within the naval acoustic environment in past decades.

On the other hand, from their initial participation, women in the combat arms have represented relatively sudden and permanent change to an extensive history of an exclusively male cultural domain. For centuries many women have participated in armed conflict, met significant physical challenges, and faced extremely harsh conditions, including the threat and reality of violent death, in war and many other situations. Yet the full and permanent status of women as members of combat military organizations such as regiments is very new. Individual success under such demanding social and historical conditions demands leadership. The women who enter are dependent upon leaders who can effectively lead a mixed gender team. Also, by virtue of the fact that the presence of women is still unique in the combat environment, women must be able to effectively negotiate the reactions and opinions of peers, leaders, and subordinates, in reference to the suitability of women in the combat domain. From day one, women must exercise effective leadership qualities to succeed. The demand for leadership ability at relatively junior and inexperienced levels can be paramount for women in gender-isolated roles and domains.

Indeed, the research that was conducted in 1997 on the experience of women in the combat arms concluded that those women who had the most positive experiences in the combat arms "demonstrated an extraordinary understanding"[60] of male group processes and how these processes impacted interpretations of women's performance and social activity. These women attributed persistent stereotyping of women's social behaviour in particular to the masculine combat arms culture, rather than as personal attacks on their character and reputation.[61] This experience also reinforces the importance for leaders to understand the broader social processes that impact the status of women in the military.

As the CF strives to strengthen the fragile status of women in the combat arms, it is also facing an increasingly complex range of defence demands. In 2006 in Afghanistan, the CF experienced combat casualties, including the first woman in combat, at a rate unprecedented since the Korean War. The Canadian response to the death of Captain Nichola Goddard on May 17, 2006 in a battle with the Taliban raised few questions in reference to appropriate roles and the experience of women in the military. Instead, there was an overwhelming focus on the fact that Canada had lost a competent, dedicated soldier, regardless of whether male or female.[62] However, a recent article in the *Ottawa Citizen* did highlight the fact that female soldiers are "writing a new chapter in Canadian military history, taking on high-profile roles on the front lines in Afghanistan",[63] and are thus "shoving aside misconceptions about whether women are equipped for war",[64] and whether their presence will affect the chemistry of previously all-male units".[65] The reporter notes that she was not able to find anyone who was aware of any research being done on women in the combat arms. This, of course, leads to questions of what kind of research or initiatives might be required and what questions should the CF be asking about the experience of women in the combat arms. It is widely accepted that Canadian defence objectives will most effectively be met with the full participation of a demographically diverse Canadian society – not just in terms of numbers, but also in terms of full participation and integration into all organizational processes. As a minimum, it is important to ensure that the CF learns from the experiences of women just as it learns from the experiences of men.

Concurrent with continued progress on the gender integration front, the CF has shifted from a Cold War status to meet the challenges of the changing security environment. The CF is frequently involved in highly volatile and dangerous combat missions, along with a range of activities that have implications for integrated defence, development and diplomacy (3D) and joint, interoperable, multinational, and public (JIMP) cooperation and outcomes. It is important to understand the implications of the changing security environment for women as members of the CF, and as leaders in the CF. How has military service in the CF changed for women and men, and how can leadership continue to leverage the contributions of both women and men in an increasingly volatile, high tempo security environment? Complacency is not progress, and these are but a few of the questions that need to be answered.

ENDNOTES

1   Petty Officer 1st Class (ret'd) Leslie Crepin, Personal Communication (February 2007).

2   Naval term still used in the early 1980s for female Leading Seaman, rank equivalent to CF Corporal. Soon after, the CF directed that all Wrens would be called Leading Seaman to promote equal treatment of women and men. However, many women argued, to no avail, that calling women a seaman was less equitable than being called a Wren.

3   As a result of a complaint based on the Canadian Charter of Rights and Freedoms, homosexuals have been enrolled and retained in the Canadian Forces since 1992. For further explanation, see Franklin C. Pinch, "Canada: Managing Change with Shrinking Resources" in *The Postmodern Military: Armed Forces After the Cold War.* Charles C. Moskos, John Allen Williams, and David R. Segal (eds.) (New York and Oxford: Oxford University Press, 2000), 169.

4   Department of National Defence, Directorate of History, File 78/517; Robinson, 1988; Suzanne Simpson, Doris Toole and Cindy Player, "Women in the Canadian Forces: Past, Present and Future" *Atlantis.* 4 (II, 1979), 226-283.

5   Suzanne Simpson et al, "Women in the Canadian Forces: Past, Present and Future ".

6   Officer classifications: Aerospace Engineer; Communications/Electronics Engineer; Dental, Air Traffic Control, Air Weapons Control, Legal; and Logistics. Non-Commissioned Member trades: Photographic Technician; Air Traffic Control Assistant, Military Police, Cook, Aero-Engine Technician; Air Frame Technician; Metals Technician, Machinist; and Refinisher Technician. Public Service of Canada, 1974.

7   Suzanne Simpson et al, "Women in the Canadian Forces: Past, Present and Future ".

8   National Defence, Directorate of Information Systems 1993, Job #2146.

9   Department of National Defence, *Defence* (Ottawa, ON: Minister of Supply and Services Canada, 1980 cited in K. D. Davis, "Women and Military Service in Canada: 1885 – Present" (North York, Ontario: Canadian Forces Personnel Applied Research Unit, 1996), Historical Report 96-1.

10   Canadian Human Rights Commission, *The Canadian Human Rights Act: A Guide.* (Ottawa, ON: Minister of Supply and Services, 1988) cited in K. D. Davis, "Women and Military Service in Canada: 1885 – Present".

11   Department of National Defence, *Summary of Surveys on Women in Combat and Isolated Posting.* (Ottawa: Directorate Personnel Development Studies, 1978).

12   Ibid.

13   Ibid.

14   Rosemary E. Park, *Overview of the Social/Behavioural Science Evaluation of the 1979-1985 Canadian Forces Trial Employment of Servicewomen in Non-Traditional Environments and Roles.* (Willowdale, Ontario: Canadian Forces Personnel Applied Research Unit, 1986).

15   Ibid.

16   Ibid.

17   Rosemary E. Park, *Final Report of the Social/Behavioural Science Evaluation of the SWINTER Sea Trial.* (Willowdale, Onatrio: Canadian Forces Personnel Applied Research Unit, 1984).

18   Rosemary E. Park, *Overview of the Social/Behavioural Science Evaluation of the 1979-1985 Canadian Forces Trial Employment of Servicewomen in Non-Traditional Environments and Roles.*

19   At the time of this research, lesbians and homosexuals were prohibited from serving in the CF. However, by 1992 the courts in Canada had held that Section 15 of the Canadian Charter of Rights and Freedoms protected equality on the basis of sexual orientation, and in 1993 restrictions and barriers related to sexual orientation were removed from CF regulations. In 1996, the Canadian Human Rights Act was amended to include sexual orientation as a prohibited ground of discrimination under Section 15 of the Act (http://www.chrc-ccdp.ca/discrimination/sexual_orientation-en.asp).

20   Canadian Human Rights Commission, *Tribunal Decision 3/89 Between: ISABELLE GAUTHIER, JOSEPH G. HOULDEN, MARIE-CLAUDE GAUTHIER, GEORGINA ANN BROWN Complainants and CANADIAN ARMED FORCES Respondent* (Decision Rendered on February 20, 1989).

21   Cheryl D. Lamerson, *Integration of Women Into Previously All-Male Units: A Literature Review.* (Willowdale, Ontario: Canadian Forces Personnel Applied Research Unit, 1987).

22   Shirley M. Robinson, "The Right to Serve: Women and the 'Combat Issue', Part I" Forum. 3(1, 1988), 22-24.

23   Cheryl D. Lamerson, *Monitoring the Recruitment of Women: A Working Plan.* (Willowdale, Ontario: Canadian Forces Personnel Applied Research Unit, 1988).

24   Cheryl D. Lamerson, *Combat Related Employment of Women (CREW) in the Army: Trial Research Plan.* (Willowdale, Ontario: Canadian Forces Personnel Applied Research Unit, 1989); and Cheryl D. Lamerson, *Combat Related Employment of Women (CREW) in the Navy: Trial Research Plan.* (Willowdale, Ontario: Canadian Forces Personnel Applied Research Unit, 1989).

25   Ibid.

26   Canadian Human Rights Commission, *Tribunal Decision 3/89.*

27   Ibid.

28   Bill C-64, an Act Respecting Employment Equity, received Royal Assent in the House of Commons in December 1995, creating a new legislated framework, which included the CF. However, the Act did not apply to the CF until the Canadian Forces Employment Equity Regulations were approved by the Governor-in-Council. The CF received approval for special Canadian Forces Employment Equity Regulations 21 November 2002, and is now officially governed by the Act and subject to Canadian Human Rights Commission compliance audit.

29   Although women cannot be ordained in the Roman Catholic Church, women have been serving in the CF as Roman Catholic Pastoral Associates since 1982. Joanne Benham, Religion and Military Culture in the 21st Century, University of Waterloo, draft of an unpublished Ph.D. thesis.

30   Leesa M. Tanner and C. Walters, *Marital Status of Women in the Canadian Forces.* (Ottawa, ON: Department of National Defence, Operational Research and Analysis Establishment, Directorate of Manpower Analysis, 1990).

31   The Minister's Advisory Board on Gender Integration in the Canadian Forces, *The Minister's Advisory Board on Gender Integration in the Canadian Forces: The Fifth Annual Report Mid-Term 1989-1994* (1995).

32   Leesa M. Tanner, *Gender Integration in the Canadian Forces – A Quantitative and Qualitative Analysis.* (Ottawa, Canada: Department of National Defence, Operational Research Division Report, 1999).

33   R. O. Parker, K. M. Farley, and D. Dellabough, D., *Gender Differences in Voluntary Attrition from Hard Sea Occupations.* (Willowdale, Ontario: Canadian Forces Personnel Applied Research Unit, 1993).

34   Leesa M. Tanner and C. Walters, *Marital Status of Women in the Canadian Forces.*

35   Leesa M. Tanner, *The Career Progression of Women in the Canadian Forces - Is There A "Glass Ceiling?".* (Ottawa, Canada: Department of National Defence, Operational Research and Analysis Establishment, Directorate of Manpower Analysis, 1992).

36   Leesa M. Tanner, *Status of Trained Women in the Canadian Forces.* (Ottawa, Canada: Department of National Defence, Operational Research and Analysis Establishment, Directorate of Manpower Analysis, 1992).

37   Leesa M. Tanner, *Gender Integration in the Canadian Forces – A Quantitative and Qualitative Analysis.*

38   Karen D. Davis, *Organizational Environment and Turnover: Understanding Women's Exit From the Canadian Forces. Unpublished Master's Thesis* (Montreal, QC: McGill University, 1994).

39   R. J. Hansen, *Personal Harassment in the Canadian Forces: 1992 Survey.* (North York, Ontario: Canadian Forces Personnel Applied Research Unit, 1993).

40   Adams-Roy, J.E. 1999a. *Harassment in the Canadian Forces: Results of the 1998 Survey.* (Ottawa, Canada: Department of National Defence, Director Human Resources Research and Evaluation, 1999).

41   Nicola J. Holden and Karen D. Davis, "Harassment in the Military: Cross-National Comparisons" in *Challenge and Change in the Military: Gender and Diversity Issues* Franklin C. Pinch, Allister T. MacIntyre, Phyllis Browne, and Alan C. Okros (eds.) (Kingston, ON: Canadian Defence Academy Press, 2004, third printing 2008).

42   Ibid.

43   Karen D. Davis, *Chief Land Staff Gender Integration Study: The Regular Force Training and Employment Environment.* (Ottawa, Canada: National Defence Headquarters, Personnel Research Team, 1997).

44 Karen D. Davis and Virginia Thomas, *Chief Land Staff Gender Integration Study: The Experience of Women Who Have Served in the Combat Arms*. (Ottawa, Canada: National Defence Headquarters, Personnel Research Team, 1998).

45 Ibid.

46 Cross-Cultural/Multicultural Associates Inc., *Canadian Forces Diversity Project: Baseline Survey*. (Ottawa, Canada: Department of National Defence, Director Human Resources Research and Evaluation, 1997).

47 Karen D. Davis, *Mixed Gender Opinion Questionnaire: CF Regular Force 1997 Administration*. (Ottawa, Canada: Department of National Defence, Directorate Human Resources Research and Evaluation, 1998).

48 H. Pike and R. N. MacLennan, *Canadian Forces Diversity Climate Project: 1999 Survey*. (Ottawa, Canada: Department of National Defence, Directorate Human Resources Research and Evaluation, 2000).

49 L. Bradley, *Mixed Gender Crewing in VICTORIA Class Submarines*. (Ottawa: Department of National Defence, Chief of Maritime Staff, 1999)

50 Women cannot serve in the CF as a Roman Catholic padre, due to restrictions maintained by the Roman Catholic tradition.

51 For example, the findings presented in Michael Adams, *Sex in the Snow: Canadian Social Values at the End of the Millenium*. (Toronto, Ontario, Canada: Penguin Books Canada Ltd., 1997), was widely embraced by staff officers in National Defence Headquarters.

52 Department of National Defence, Output Products, accessed January 2007, http://hr3.ottawa-hull.mil.ca/dhrim/engraph/home_e.asp.

53 Department of National Defence, *Canadian Forces National Report to the Committee for Women in NATO Forces* (Ottawa, Canada: Director Human Rights and Diversity, 2006).

54 Includes the ranks of Major, Lieutenant-Colonel, and Colonel as well as naval equivalent ranks of Lieutenant-Commander, Commander and Captain (Navy).

55 Department of National Defence, *Output Products*, accessed January 2007, http://hr3.ottawa-hull.mil.ca/dhrim/engraph/home_e.asp.

56 Includes the ranks of Sergeant, Warrant Officer, Master Warrant Officer and Chief Warrant Officer as well as naval equivalent ranks of Petty Officer

2nd Class, Petty Officer 1st Class, Chief Petty Officer 2nd Class, and Chief Petty Officer 1st Class.

57   Department of National Defence, *Output Products*, accessed January 2007, http://hr3.ottawa-hull.mil.ca/dhrim/engraph/home_e.asp.

58   See, for example, the perspective shared by Captain Eleanor Taylor, "Women in the Battallion: A Leadership Challenge" in *In the Breach: Perspectives on Leadership in the Army Today.* Lieutenant-Colonel Bernd Horn (ed.), (Kingston, ON: Director General Land Combat Development, 2004).

59   The TAS Op occupation has recently been re-named Sonar Operator.

60   K. D. Davis and Virginia Thomas, *Chief Land Staff Gender Integration Study: The Experience of Women Who Have Served in the Combat Arms.* (Ottawa, Canada: Department of National Defence, Personnel Research Team, 1998).

61   Ibid.

62   Karen D. Davis, "Gender, Discourse, and War: Canadian Casualties of Afghanistan, 2006," (Kingston, ON: Royal Military College of Canada, 2007), unpublished paper submitted in partial fulfillment of Ph.D. course requirements.

63   Liane Faulder, "Outside the Wire" *Ottawa Citizen.* (February 4, 2007), B4.

64   Ibid.

65   Ibid.

CHAPTER 8

Gender and Leadership in the Canadian Forces Combat Arms: Perspectives of Women Leaders

Dr. Angela R. Febbraro

In 1989, a Canadian Human Rights Tribunal ordered the Canadian Forces (CF) to fully integrate women into all occupations, including the combat arms.[1] Since then, the CF has made considerable strides in gender integration. Canadian women have participated with distinction in a wide range of domestic and international military operations, from humanitarian relief to peacekeeping to war-fighting. However, although women are beginning to be appointed to senior operational leadership positions in the CF, women have not progressed in large numbers to the most senior ranks, particularly in the combat arms, where women account for only 3.9 percent of officers and 1.4 percent of non-commissioned members (NCMs).[2] Perhaps of greatest concern, the attrition rate for women in the combat arms has been high; in fact, in some cases six times higher than the rate for men.[3]

Previous scientific research has suggested that one explanation for the slow progress of women into leadership positions in general involves the critical role that gender stereotyping plays in leadership appraisals and concepts.[4] Despite numerous studies showing women's leadership effectiveness, and only small gender differences in leadership style,[5] there is still the widespread belief, first demonstrated over 30 years ago,[6] that women are not suited for leadership positions, and the stereotype of "effective leader" remains masculine in content.[7] Indeed, numerous studies suggest that there exists a strong cultural association between traditional notions of masculinity and concepts of leadership, including military leadership.[8] In the CF, for example, stereotypes about leaders may include physical characteristics (e.g., tall, broad-shouldered, loud voice), behaviours (e.g., touching or other nonverbal behaviour during interpersonal interactions, conversational styles), and other attributes (e.g., interests, participation in specific social rituals), which may exclude women but actually have little to do with effective leadership.[9] Indeed, although the scientific literature has demonstrated women's leadership effectiveness in many settings, one noteworthy exception has been the military context. Eagly, Karau, and Makhijani's[10] meta-analytic review of 76 studies of leadership effectiveness in the military setting, for instance, concluded that women performed less effectively than men in this context. However, this gender difference was found even when the sexes engaged in equivalent leadership behaviours, suggesting that the gender difference reflects a gender stereotype or bias rather than a true performance difference. A similar finding was obtained more recently by Boldry, Wood and Kashy,[11] in their study of women and men in the Texas A&M Corps of Cadets: Men more than women were judged to possess the motivation and leadership qualities necessary for effective military performance (e.g., competitiveness, physical fitness, independence, self-confidence), whereas women were believed to possess more feminine attributes that impair effective leadership performance (e.g., being helpful, kind, gentle, and emotionally expressive) – despite the fact that men and women did not differ on objective measures of military leadership performance.[12]

Eagly, Karau, and Makhijani[13] have offered *role congruity theory* as an explanation for the gender stereotyping of leadership positions and its effects. According to this theory, perceptions of the appropriate roles for the two genders may conflict with expectations regarding leadership roles, especially when an occupation is held predominantly by one sex. For example, women leaders may be evaluated negatively when they violate gender-role expectations by adopting masculine leadership behaviours and failing to exhibit "feminine" leadership behaviours in a male-dominated context.[14] Role congruity theory also suggests, however, that the "male managerial model" may pose barriers for women who aspire to leadership positions, because if women engage in feminine behaviours in accordance with their gender role, then they may be seen as unable to behave in a way congruent with appropriate leadership behaviours. As noted above, however, even when women engage in the same (masculine) leadership behaviours as men, women may also be evaluated negatively. As a whole, previous research results reflect the dilemma that women leaders face. On the one hand, women may not be perceived as leaders simply by virtue of their gender – unless, perhaps, they act in masculine ways. On the other hand, when women do act in masculine ways (e.g., autocratically), their performance ratings may suffer, especially if they are being rated by men in a male-dominated environment. This "catch-22" seems especially pertinent to the military context, where attributes of masculinity have traditionally been encouraged. Indeed, the psychological attributes required of a successful soldier or military leader (decisiveness, confidence, assertiveness), are also stereotypic of men, whereas the stereotypic qualities possessed by women (kindness, emotional expressiveness) are explicitly rejected.[15]

Previous Canadian Forces Research on Women in the Combat Arms

Echoing the findings on gender and leadership cited above, previous CF research on women who left the combat arms[16] has identified a number of social-psychological barriers to gender integration. Based on interviews with 31 women who left the combat arms (including 6 officers), Davis and Thomas[17] found that even where official policies permitted women to be employed, and even where women met physical standards, women reported numerous social and psychological barriers which affected their ability to perform and which had a significant impact on whether or not they were deemed suitable for the combat arms or leadership roles. According to Davis and Thomas, the very fact that they were women in a male-defined and male-dominated environment resulted in ambiguous perceptions and beliefs on the part of peers and supervisors regarding women's abilities and motivation as leaders/combat soldiers. Further, Davis and Thomas reported that women felt that they had to become "one of the guys" if they were to succeed; yet, a woman's motivation to take on a "male role" was also suspect, reflecting, once again, a difficult dilemma for women in such contexts.

In another study, Davis[18] conducted 49 focus groups with 344 men and women in the combat arms, combat support, and combat service support environments, and concluded that women face considerable challenges within the Regular Force combat arms training and employment environment. Concerning leadership, male junior combat arms officers in training expressed the belief that women cannot be effective leaders, as they do not possess "command presence".[19] The men did not believe that the troops would have confidence in a woman's ability to lead, and, therefore, would not follow her. In addition, female participants expressed the belief that women's ability to perform in leadership roles is questioned and compromised. The end result, according to Davis,[20] is that women in the combat arms are accorded less respect and support in their roles as leaders than are their male counterparts.

The findings of Davis[21] are similar to those reported by Yoder,[22] who studied the experiences of the first women cadets to attend the United States Military Academy at West Point, a training ground for military leaders. Yoder[23] found that instead of learning to be leaders, the women cadets became passive observers who were often criticized for their "noncommand voices" and peripheral importance.[24] Almost half of the women in Yoder's study reported feeling overprotected as cadets, a circumstance incompatible with the leadership role but one that conforms readily to the feminine role. Yoder found that in a setting that defined cadets in masculine terms, the women struggled to create a new role, that of "woman-cadet," but also to disassociate themselves from femininity. As an example of the latter, women shunned their skirted uniforms and instead tried to blend in by wearing only trousers.[25] Once again, such behaviours reflect the dilemmas that women face as they negotiate their leadership roles in military contexts.

The research studies by Davis and colleagues,[26] and by Yoder[27] were conducted several years ago, leaving open questions as to what the more contemporary experience is like for women leaders in the combat arms. Do they still face dilemmas and other social-psychological barriers related to gender and leadership? Are their experiences and perspectives on gender and leadership any different from those of the women who left the combat arms according to Davis' 1997 study? The present chapter will address some of these questions by focusing on the perspectives and experiences of women leaders in the CF combat arms regarding several issues pertaining to gender and leadership. These issues include: the meaning of effective leadership according to the women, and whether this is perceived as gendered by the women; their own personal leadership style; personal strategies used by the women for enhancing their own leadership effectiveness; resistance to women in leadership roles that the women have encountered and how they have dealt with this resistance; the ways in which the women leaders feel that they have impacted military culture; and the positive leadership practices, as well as the organizational/CF policies and practices that the women feel can enhance gender integration.

Participants

Participants were eight female leaders employed in the Regular Force combat arms (i.e., infantry, armoured, artillery, and combat engineer) occupations at 2 Canadian Mechanized Brigade Group (2 CMBG), Canadian Forces Base (CFB) Petawawa. These eight women were part of a larger study that included 26 women in combat arms occupations at CFB Petawawa.[28] At the time of the study, the leaders (i.e., officers) were either lieutenants or captains, most were in their 20s, and all had at least a university education. Although all had had command appointments at some point in their careers, fewer than half had been deployed, either domestically or overseas. The modal number of years of military or combat arms experience was four to six years, although some participants had more than 10 years of military or combat arms experience.

Prior to their participation, potential participants received an information letter describing the study, which stated that the goal of the research was to "contribute to a better and more up-to-date understanding of women in the combat arms, particularly in relation to leadership issues", and a list of interview questions. Prior to the start of their interview, participants were briefed on the objectives and potential benefits of the study, the nature of their participation (e.g., format, time commitment), and confidentiality issues (e.g., it was emphasized that if interview excerpts were to be used in reports or publications, under no circumstances would identifying characteristics be included). Participants then signed an informed voluntary consent form indicating their willingness to participate and to be tape-recorded and quoted in reports or publications of the research. Participants were also asked to complete a biographical data form prior to the commencement of the interview in order to obtain relevant demographic data (e.g., age, education, rank, number of years in the military/combat arms, current position, command/leadership positions held, deployments). No incentives for participation, remuneration or compensation of any kind were used in this study.

Research Approach

In-depth, one-on-one interviews were conducted in person by the author in February and May 2003. The interviews were semi-structured in format and averaged about one hour in length. The main categories of topics explored in the interview included experiences in the CF/combat arms, women and leadership in the CF/combat arms, and gender integration in the CF/combat arms. More specifically, the interview explored: the women's perspectives on the definition of effective leadership and whether this definition was perceived by the women as gendered (e.g., whether effective leadership was considered masculine or feminine, or whether effective leadership was defined differently for women and men); the women's accounts of their own personal leadership style; the personal strategies used by the women for enhancing their own leadership effectiveness; any resistance to women in leadership roles that the women experienced and how they dealt with this resistance; the ways in which the women leaders felt that they have impacted military culture; the positive leadership practices that the women felt may promote gender integration; and the organizational/CF policies and practices that the women felt may facilitate gender integration.

Following a naturalistic paradigm,[29] interviews were transcribed and coded into thematic areas corresponding to specific research issues, using the NUD*IST qualitative software (Non-numerical Unstructured Data with Indexing, Searching and Theorizing, version N6). Based a consensus in the literature regarding what constitutes masculine and feminine characteristics,[30] *masculine* leadership characteristics were defined (or *coded*) as those characteristics that are agentic or task-oriented in nature (e.g., decisive, unemotional, aggressive, directive), and *feminine* leadership characteristics were defined as those characteristics that are communal or person-oriented in nature (e.g., compassionate, emotionally expressive, concerned with others, participative). Briefly, three basic steps were followed for the analysis, based on Patton's[31] abbreviated form of content analysis: organizing the data, which consisted of reading the content of each interview; grouping or *coding* all comments into relevant categories (e.g., the main issues of interest, such as perceptions of what behaviours, abilities, or characteristics constitute effective leadership); and noting variations in opinions based on different factors. To illustrate dominant themes and patterns, excerpts from interviews are presented.[32] In addition, a quantitative description of the data is also included in the discussion below (e.g., frequency counts, percentages), as appropriate.

Perspectives on Effective Leadership: To Be Masculine, Feminine, or Androgynous?

When asked to reflect generally on their views regarding what characteristics constitute effective leadership, all eight leaders reported feeling that *both* masculine (task-oriented) and feminine (person-oriented) characteristics are needed, and referred to both of these categories of behaviours or traits in their accounts of leadership effectiveness. This suggests that the women leaders in this study do not define effective leadership in strictly masculine *or* feminine terms, but see value in *both* styles of leadership.[33] For instance, all eight leaders mentioned *masculine* traits as being important for leadership effectiveness. One officer emphasized the importance of maintaining emotional control, for example, by not crying during difficult situations:

> Somebody who cries under pressure...I think will undermine the way the soldiers perceive them. ...I don't think you should cry in front of subordinates, ever. ... ...If you can't control your emotions in a day-to-day office environment or in a training environment, how are you possibly going to hold things together when your best friend is dying beside you? So I do think emotional control is very important.

As was the case regarding masculine traits, all eight leaders also identified *feminine* traits, such as having good communication skills, as being important for leadership effectiveness.

One officer spoke of the importance of showing compassion and being a good listener so that you are able to understand what your soldiers needs are, and "understand what they are saying, even if they are not saying it". Another officer observed that the best leaders that she had seen, men and women, were intuitive. Still another officer spoke of the importance of a leader establishing a connection with her or his soldiers to be effective as a leader. Moreover, each one of the eight leaders talked about leadership effectiveness in what could be described as *androgynous* terms; that is, they mentioned *both* masculine and feminine traits in their descriptions of effective leadership, often in close juxtaposition:

> [Effective leaders] need intellect, intuition, common sense, a sense of humour and some backbone. That's what you need.

In the excerpt below, the officer speaks of the importance of a leader both listening (a feminine trait) and taking action to solve problems (a masculine trait):

> …You have to be willing to learn and to listen. And when the troops see that you're listening to them in something like tactics, they will be able to come to you with something personal, or a problem, because they'll know that you'll listen. And you also have to be very active. If someone comes to you with something, you make sure that it gets done and you follow up on it. … And you follow up on it until it's resolved because you just don't let them hang, you know, my buddy's Private Married Quarter (PMQ) has no windows. …You keep bugging people until you get a window.

Some leaders were explicit about the importance of applying different leadership styles to different situations, an ability which androgynous leaders, who combine both masculine and feminine traits, possess. The excerpt below is from an officer who distinguished between the (masculine) war-fighting skills (e.g., aggression, a command-based style) needed during phase training, and the (feminine) administrative skills needed in battalion (e.g., peace-support, a co-operative style):

> ...The style that you employ on phase training is different from the style that you actually should employ when you're in a battalion. ... When you're on phase training...you're...very much assessed on your ability to give aggressive commands, because you're also practicing war-fighting skills. When you get to the battalion...you may be... practicing for peacekeeping, things like that, and you have to adopt a more co-operative style as opposed to a command-based style.

Another officer spoke of the need to be able to use a variety of leadership styles, that is, to be more directive in certain situations, and more consultative in others:

> ...You have to be prepared to use a variety of styles. And you have to be...aware of when...what style is fitting. You have to be prepared to say no, I told you what I want and you're going to do it now. Or, all right, I guess we could do it your way. ... It depends on the situation, whether you're more directive or whether you're more consultative perhaps.

Similarly, another officer expressed the view that a leader need not be loud, assertive, or aggressive in every situation in order to be effective, and that sometimes a calmer approach may be more appropriate. This same officer quoted above went on to say that, depending on the situation, emotionality also has its place in leadership effectiveness:

> Obviously you're going to be more emotional in certain situations, if you're dealing with soldiers who are having family problems or personal problems. I think there is a time to show your more emotional or caring or nurturing side and obviously there's not a place for that on the battlefield when you're giving orders and you're, you know, so it definitely is situational. ... There's a time and a place to be emotional or aggressive for that matter.

In summary, the leaders in this study identified both masculine and feminine characteristics as constituting effective leadership. Indeed, most leaders saw value in a leader possessing both masculine and feminine traits, characteristics which could be applied flexibly to different circumstances. In other words, whether implicitly or explicitly, most leaders spoke of effective leadership in *androgynous* terms, as *integrating* both masculine and feminine characteristics.

Perspectives on Effective Leadership: Gendered, or Gender-neutral?

Participants were also asked whether or not they felt that effective leadership is defined differently for women and men, that is, whether or not they thought that the gender of the leader plays a role in defining leadership effectiveness. Among the eight leaders, three clearly felt that gender plays a role in defining effective leadership. For example, the two leaders quoted below suggested that women leaders may have something rather unique and positive to offer the military, such as their communication skills and nurturing qualities, which they believed men leaders are less likely to possess:

> I don't think we're the same as men. I don't think that we lead in the same way in general as men. … I do think that many women offer different things to the combat arms than I think they're maybe a little more understanding to certain personal issues, just kind of our nurturing side kind of comes out…

In contrast, the leader quoted below perceived a limitation for women leaders in comparison to men leaders, in terms of being less vocally forceful; that is, "It's hard though because I know that as a female you can't go out there and like scream at the guys like the guys do."

Five of the eight leaders gave less straightforward responses regarding the gendering of leadership. For example, the leader quoted below indicated at one point that there exists a gender difference between what constitutes effective leadership for women and men leaders, and that women should not try to behave in masculine ways because this strategy does not work:

> Maybe it works for the young male officers to look at a captain
> or a major and pick up some things from how he does it and un-
> consciously or consciously try and do it that way, and have that role
> model. But for women it doesn't. You look silly. You look like you're
> trying to be someone that you're not. You look like you're trying to
> be a man. ... You look like you're wearing someone else's suit. And
> it doesn't mean that you can't do it. You just have to figure how it
> works for women. ... Just be comfortable in your own shoes.

However, in other parts of the conversation, this leader emphasized the
similarity between women and men in their leadership qualities:

> It's not true that men are not empathetic or caring and women are.
> Those are good leadership qualities and they are absolutely there
> with men. So, I'd say it's a...trait issue rather than what females are
> good at and what males are good at. ... And there's no difference
> I believe between a good male leader and a good female leader.
> They exhibit the same characteristics. It's just the definition of this
> is being male and this is being female that are probably not in my
> mind appropriate.

In short, many of the leaders in this study indicated, in various ways, that
gender does play a role in defining leadership effectiveness. Although many
accounts were rather equivocal with respect to the "gendering of leadership,"
many of the women indicated that gender made a difference, whether in
terms of differences in leadership style or qualities, or in terms of differences
in what it takes to be perceived as an effective leader.

Personal Leadership Styles

In reflecting upon their own styles of leadership, all eight leaders in this study
described their own leadership style in integrative terms, as drawing on or
integrating both masculine and feminine characteristics. For instance, the
leader quoted below described how, in developing her leadership style, she
integrates her ability to discipline soldiers with her listening skills:

I'm, tend to be fairly laid back with things that come up... Even when I've had to discipline guys or whatever, I'd rather talk about it, listen to what they have to say, and then sort it out.

Similarly, the leader quoted below described how she integrates her ability to understand people with her aggressive skills:

I believe that primarily as a leader I try to know and understand those people that I work with, and motivate them according to their personalities. At times I have to be aggressive. Certainly in a field environment. ... But I don't believe you always have to be like that.

Furthermore, several leaders emphasized the importance of their feminine attributes (e.g., interpersonal skills) to developing an effective leadership style. For example, they mentioned being intuitive; they mentioned the gratification they experienced through developing followers; and they mentioned their approachability, their ability to read and understand others, and their ability to listen. These themes are reflected in the following quotations. In the first quotation below, the leader is remarking on her interpersonal skills, and the great sense of satisfaction that she receives from interacting with people, reflecting a *person-orientation*:

[I've been described as] very approachable. ... Troops aren't afraid to come and talk to [me]. ... I like talking to people, I like interacting with people. ... I think it has to be my...greatest satisfaction. ... One of my best skills I think is my ability to read people and their strengths and weaknesses, basically to assess people and [I like] the fact that I get to...use it a lot in this profession.

In the next quotation, a leader is describing the sense of satisfaction she receives from developing or *empowering* others:

I'm trying to develop the subordinates underneath me, so working with others and then working and helping improve others. ... And seeing them progress through. [It's a gratifying experience.]

In the quotation below, the leader described her leadership style as *participative*, in that she is willing to make concessions to others so that ultimately things may go better and smoother:

> I always thought myself as very much more participative than, you know, this is the way we're going now, unless we're in a situation where we have tight timelines, we need something done. ... So... I'm willing to make concessions to make somebody else feel happier even though I may not think it's going to be as effective that way. ... Because at the end of the day, if we're both on the same side, we're going to go better and we're going to go smoother.

Similarly, another leader considered herself to be "more of a democratic leader", particularly when it came to making decisions and receiving input from others to formulate her plans.

Thus, once again, the accounts of the women leaders in this study regarding their own leadership styles suggest that they do not define effective leadership in strictly masculine *or* feminine terms, but see value in possessing both masculine and feminine characteristics that could be applied flexibly to different circumstances. Indeed, the women leaders in this study have been adopting alternative styles of leadership – styles that are more feminine (person-oriented, empowering, participative, and democratic) – not to the exclusion of masculine characteristics but *in addition* to such characteristics. In short, most leaders spoke of effective leadership, including their own leadership, as *integrating* both masculine and feminine characteristics. As will be discussed in a later section of this chapter, such an integrative approach to leadership provides evidence of gender integration in the CF combat arms.

Personal Strategies for Enhancing Leadership Effectiveness

The women leaders in this study also talked about other strategies that they used for enhancing their own leadership effectiveness. In particular, they spoke explicitly about whether or not they felt that they must act in masculine ways in order to be perceived as an effective leader by others. Among the eight leaders, six did *not* feel that they must adopt a masculine leadership style in order to be perceived as an effective leader. Instead, they emphasized the importance of being themselves, and of developing their own leadership style, rather than trying to imitate a masculine leadership style. The following four quotations are from leaders who illustrated this theme. The first is from a leader who, after struggling with the question of whether or not to adopt a masculine leadership style, ultimately decided that every leader must develop her or his *own* leadership style:

> I struggled [with] should I be adopting a masculine leadership style? And the answer, for everybody, is adopt your own leadership style. Find out what works for you. ... At times I have to be aggressive. In a field environment, you've got to be that yeller and screamer and you've got to give that decisive direction at that time. But I don't believe you always have to be like that. In fact, I think it works better if you're not always like that.

Initially, the leader quoted below felt that she must change her style in order to be considered an effective leader in the combat arms; however, after gaining some experience, she concluded that she did *not* have to change her leadership style:

> [Previously]...I tried to be abrupt and abrasive and that didn't work very well. And then you just try to be yourself and you don't have any problems. ... I don't think [female leaders have to] change, no.

Another leader felt that there was even a place for femininity in the combat arms, and that it was not necessary to become more masculine in order to be seen as effective by others:

> I wouldn't say that women should ever try to be more masculine. I think that there's a place for femininity in the combat arms, and I don't think that we have to be masculine to be successful...

Still another experienced a great sense of relief once she discovered that she could be herself, rather than someone who screams and yells, and still be considered an effective leader:

I had my reservations about the yelling and screaming kind of flamboyant style, and when I got here and I realized that they don't require that at all and they don't like it, I was like, ah, great, that's perfect, because now I can be myself, and I can be more natural and not have to put on this kind of persona that wasn't me or a style that wasn't me and I didn't like.

In contrast, the leader cited below expressed the view that it was necessary, in certain respects, to adopt a masculine style in order to be perceived as an effective leader:

You do in some senses [need to behave in a masculine way in order to be perceived to be an effective soldier]. … I don't think it's positive to be too feminine, quote unquote. I mean, you can't spend hours doing make-up or anything like that. … You do have to have a certain degree of…non-sexuality about you.

In addition to the issue of whether or not it was necessary to "act like a man" in order to be perceived as an effective leader, leaders also talked about other strategies for enhancing their own leadership effectiveness. For instance, one leader emphasized the general importance of doing a good job and caring for your troops:

…As long as you're doing your job and you look after them, they're not going to care if you're male, female… If you're doing your job as a troop leader, there isn't really a difference in their eyes between men and women.

However, the same leader quoted above also emphasized the importance of behaving like a professional, especially as a woman, suggesting that women leaders in the combat arms, at least in some respects, may still be under greater scrutiny than their male counterparts, a theme to which we shall return:

I think it's better to remain professional. That's why I don't go out and get completely hammered. Especially as a woman. I mean, there's horror stories around the base of female officers sleeping with their troops or getting involved and this and that. …You do have to be yourself and if you want to go out and party and drink it up, that's fine, but you still have to remain professional and that builds the trust…

Thus, women leaders in the combat arms have developed personal strategies for enhancing their own leadership effectiveness. They strive to integrate both masculine and feminine characteristics and, moreover, they seek to develop a personal leadership style that fits their own unique qualities in authentic ways, as opposed to trying to imitate others' (or masculine) leadership styles. Above all, they place a high priority on caring for the well being of their soldiers and on being professionals, both of which are keys to effective leadership.

Resistance to Women in Leadership Roles in the Combat Arms

Even as the women in this study spoke positively of their strategies for developing effective leadership styles – and even as several women spoke passionately about the satisfactions and rewards that they experienced in their careers in the combat arms and felt, overall, that gender integration was proceeding smoothly – many of the women in this study also spoke of various forms of resistance that they encountered as women leaders in the combat arms. For instance, the leader quoted below reported experiencing no problems with subordinates or with non-commissioned officers (NCOs), but did report encountering some difficulties with male peers during her phase training, who apparently were uncomfortable with having to compete with a female:

I personally have never had a problem with subordinates or even NCOs from a leadership style. I find them to be very accepting. They don't care, as long as you're competent in your job it really doesn't matter to them. I found more difficulties with peers having a problem with a female… A lot of guys on course had a problem with that… It's more with your peers being competitive with you.

Similarly, another leader talked about how well she got along with her subordinates and about how much she enjoyed her job, but she still encountered gender stereotypes (e.g., about women being more emotional or less physically able than men). This leader also talked about how she addressed these stereotypes. In regard to women's supposed emotionality, she argued that emotionality could be a good thing, and that besides, men can also be emotional. In regard to women's physical abilities, she argued that one way to address this issue is to set one physical standard for women and men:

> I've had no problems with any of my subordinates, like we get along fine... I don't think they have a problem working for a woman, and I really enjoy my job. ... [But] those arguments are still definitely there...that women are more emotional than men. I mean, there are women that are very emotional but there are men that are, too. ... And maybe being somewhat more emotional is not such a bad thing, that you actually bring those points out and make those things a little bit easier to talk about. ... Yes, there probably are many women that are [physically] too weak to do certain jobs. ... But I think if we had that one standard, that would get rid of a lot of the concerns...

Furthermore, the citation below expresses one leader's perception that women in the combat arms are now treated almost too well, and that they are currently being over-accommodated and over-protected. Still, she reiterated that she *personally* has not experienced any gender-related resistance, despite having heard stories about other women's negative experiences in the combat arms:

> I would say that we are treated very well, and sometimes I feel almost too well, is becoming a bit more of the problem... I would say that a lot of people overcompensate now and sometimes it seems like there is some unfair treatment... ...I think a very kind of protective nature... Whereas with men they might do one thing but with women, oh, we got to make sure we guide her right through this. ... It just seems that it's almost gone the other way where you heard all these horror stories going through training that women

were treated horribly in the combat arms and stuff, and then you get to the unit and it's like the other way. ... So I haven't encountered any real negative myself. I've heard stories but I haven't encountered anything and I think that for the most part...people are starting to accept the fact that we are going to have women.

Another leader, quoted below, also warned against over-protecting women (e.g., by giving them clerk or similar positions), as it may lead to women not getting the field experience they need to advance in their careers. Although possibly well intentioned, this type of over-protection, as the leader explains below, ultimately works against women's career interests, and in that sense could be seen as a form of resistance to women in the combat arms:

I have seen so many females end up in the library or in clerk positions in the unit where it's an engineer position but you're the driver or the this or the that, but not out there getting the real field experience. And the problem is, because you're putting the woman into these positions, being nice to them so they're not getting the hard field experience and some of the women are pushing for this, too. ... They're not getting the necessary experience to make them good section second-in-command, to make them good section commanders. So you then end up with this kind of somewhat self-defeating cycle.

Although the majority of the women leaders in this study felt that they did not have to adopt a masculine leadership approach in order to be seen as effective, the leader quoted below did encounter, while on phase training, rather explicit resistance from a male warrant officer, who demanded that she "act like a boy" if she wanted to "play with the boys." She reported that this was the only time, in her experience in the military, that she encountered such an incident. In terms of addressing the warrant officer's resistance, she simply dismissed what he had to say, and never took his advice about acting like a boy:

[A warrant officer] proceeds to tell me that if I want to play with the boys I better start acting like one. And he doesn't agree with me being here but he can't do anything about it, so just start acting like a boy, and that was it. … I just thought he was an ignorant asshole… and I will never, ever see him as anything but a bigot and totally old-fashioned and unwilling to change. … That's the only thing I've ever had in the entire time I've been in the military.

Along the same lines, one form of resistance to women in leadership roles was expressed in this study in terms of negative implications of women leaders adopting feminine styles of leadership. In fact, four of the eight leaders spoke about negative implications associated with a female leader in the combat arms exhibiting feminine traits. For instance, the quote below is from a leader who warned against a female leader adopting feminine roles (e.g., bringing food to subordinates) or having a feminine physical appearance:

You know, it's not necessary to bring in muffins to your subordinates or to, you know, you're not supposed to paint your nails, like guys aren't supposed to paint their nails, right? There's a dress standard and you follow it. … It's not looked upon too highly, probably more harshly by the females than by the males I'd say because whenever a female officer I find does something wrong, it reflects negatively on all of us. [A woman leader who acts in a very feminine way is probably not perceived] as effective as someone who wasn't acting that way I guess. Just because it's not the place here, you know what I mean, it's just not an accepted norm I guess.

Similar views regarding feminine appearance were expressed by another leader, quoted below. This leader also warned other female leaders against displaying their sexuality or being seen as sexual objects:

…You do have to have a certain degree of, kind of non-sexuality about you. …At social functions, you're not out there to be dressed in your sexiest clothes and be, you know… … If you don't want men to think a certain way, and as a leader in the combat arms, you don't want men to think a certain way, you cannot dress like that when you go to a military social function.

In short, although leaders viewed feminine characteristics (e.g., compassion, approachability) as being important leadership attributes, some of them also perceived negative outcomes for female leaders who act in feminine ways or appear "too feminine."[34] This theme also speaks to the continued existence of a "catch-22" for female leaders. The excerpt below reflects the dilemma expressed by a leader between being perceived as too aggressive ("butch") versus too timid:

> ... As a female you can't go out there and like scream at the guys like the guys do...or you'd have to watch how you do it because then you're seen as kind of like a butch or somebody who you know is a bit too aggressive for being a female. But at the same time you can't be [very timid in your leadership approach]. ... You got to be assertive, you got to yell at the guys.

Still other women leaders in this study talked about other forms of gender-related resistance that they experienced. One woman reported failing a training course specifically, she felt, because she was a woman (she also reported that the same thing happened to another woman in the same course):

> ... I strongly believe that I failed the course because I was a woman. ... So there are still lots of people out there who are narrow-minded and it's not good that they remain in the training system, but that is one of the things that you deal with, because training systems are flawed.

Still another form of resistance can be seen in the greater scrutiny that the women in this study experienced on occasion, as minorities in a male-dominated environment. The quotation below illustrated this theme:

> When I went through training it was still very new...and so you were, like any minority, scrutinized a little bit more heavily. ... And whether or not you're actually scrutinized, you feel that you're being scrutinized. ... So, that can cause more stress and that can make it sometimes more difficult to perform.

Some of the women leaders talked about how they felt singled out by the media, which can affect how they are viewed by their subordinates, as explained by the leader quoted below:

> We were out in [location] and the media jumped all over me. Well, they're not jumping over troop leader X, who's male, and to my guys, they don't even notice a difference and then suddenly they do.

Similarly, some of the women leaders talked about being selected for certain roles (e.g., to assist with gender diversity programs) simply because they were women. The woman quoted below, who had had such an experience, held the view that as women prove their competence and as people get used to seeing women in the military, any remaining resistance to women in the military/combat arms or as leaders will diminish.

> Since I got to the unit, [my gender] hasn't really been an issue. There have been minor things which have come up. When I was first at the unit they wanted an officer to run Gender Integration… and I was the one. That's the only time I ever had to do anything I think directly related to being female. … People see women in the military more, they see competent women, women you know kind of prove themselves.

Similarly, some of the women emphasized the importance of proving themselves physically in order to prove themselves as leaders to their troops and, thus, to address any resistance to women leaders:

> If you fall out of PT [physical training], you're not leading PT. And you may never have to run operationally in your job, but my goodness, if you fall out and the troops see that, that's just not good.

In a similar vein, the following leader argued that resistance to women in the combat arms will diminish once women have proven themselves (e.g., in battle), over the long term:

Until women have been given the opportunity either through combat or through a good performance over a long period of time, they will still be looked at with scepticism. So we either need that time or we need some combat to prove our mettle.

Still other forms of resistance identified by the women included the sexual rumours (reported by one participant) and the sexist jokes that women were sometimes subjected to, at times by their own leaders. The women leader cited below, who, in another part of the conversation, had said that she had not experienced anything negative, nevertheless talked about being subjected to sexist jokes by her superior officers in front of her subordinates. Although she described these jokes as "harmless," she also felt that their continued repetition could compromise the confidence of her subordinates in her, as well as centring women out, and being potentially degrading:

> There are certain superior officers that make the odd joke still and I think it really is harmless, but when you constantly make those same jokes…about myself in front of my subordinates, well, what kind of confidence is that instilling in the subordinates? … It at least centres the woman out and it also kind of degrades them, depending on the context of the jokes obviously, but it could be degrading.

The woman who reported being the subject of sexual rumours, however, spoke passionately about how it is the responsibility of leaders to squash these types of rumours, for they can be very damaging to the women involved:

> I mention this story is because it really for me hit home the damage that simple comments, especially from superiors, can…produce, and what a failure in leadership that was. They failed as an example to their subordinates and they failed as a leader to me. … But again, it was an experience that made me think how important it is for leaders to squash that kind of thing. … As leaders it's really important for us to understand the damage that they can cause and to not allow them and certainly not start them.

Still, the woman quoted above felt that her experience as a woman leader in the combat arms has been, overall, positive:

> I don't want to leave the impression that my training experience was negative because I had some first-rate examples especially from senior NCOs that completely…, if they had any bias, they never let it show, they treated me as everybody else. Overall I learned a lot from my phase training experiences and a few negative ones that go in there every now and then.

Indeed, many of the women leaders in this study shared this perspective on their experiences in the combat arms. In general, they saw the combat arms as mostly accepting of women, but felt that it still contained elements of resistance. Still, despite some of the negative experiences that the women shared, the emphasis for most of the women leaders remained positive:

> [My training experience was] absolutely great… I had a warrant officer who is still my example of what a leader should be. He was perceptive, he was intelligent, he was demanding, he was funny, he was everything that I wanted to be as a leader. … After that my experiences just continued to get better.

Impacting Military Culture

The women in this study also shared their perspectives on how the military, including military culture, has changed with the inclusion of women in the combat arms. One leader spoke of how physical equipment or kit has changed to accommodate women's bodies, and that kit items such as the web belt was adjustable and thus suitable to various body types. Several of the leaders talked about how the inclusion of women in the combat arms has brought a greater sense of understanding, offers a new perspective, or brings an ability to communicate and connect with others. For example,

> It could be coincidence but I think that people feel more like they can let their guard down a bit. They don't have to be the big macho guy in front of the female perhaps. … We offer different perspectives

because we've been socialized or raised differently. We're wired differently if you will. So we analyze things from a different angle… and that offers something that males can't necessarily offer.

One leader described how certain traditions at mess dinners have changed with the inclusion of women, but feels that some of the men have bemoaned these changes, and that the combat arms are still, in some respects, an "old boys club:"

> It is still very much…an old boys club. And especially you go to mess dinners and you socialize with all these men and they have set traditions that they clearly haven't thought of with respect to having women in the unit. … They used to do this thing where they'd run to something naked down the street and then drink a beer. … What woman in their right mind wants to do that at a mess dinner? …Even just sitting around smoking cigars, and again I'm probably being stereotypical, but I don't know too many women that smoke cigars and that was a thing that was done at mess dinners, and some of the traditions are changing and I think that…more so the older guys that really like these traditions kind of hold a grudge towards the fact that some of these change. …They get a little sour at times… Ah, everything's changed now that we have women. You do still hear comments like that.

The same leader quoted above also spoke about how a more diverse military (which includes diverse cultures as well as women) requires new leadership competencies, such as flexibility, adaptability, and openness to diverse needs:

> …We have more of a cross-section now of society and that cross-section includes various ethnic groups, races, religions, as well as more educated individuals. … So leaders have to think out their actions a bit more and be that much more knowledgeable and competent because their soldiers are that way. And I think you have to be more situationally oriented as opposed to this is the way we're doing it and you have to be able to be a bit more reactive and

flexible. I think flexibility is a very important thing right now in leaders, because...they're a diverse set of soldiers that...we work with so you have to be able to adapt to their needs... So we have to be a bit more open to some of those things.

Still (similar to a theme we saw earlier), this leader went on to say that women should not be "over-accommodated," and therefore, centred out:

Sometimes... I think we do over-accommodate [women]. ... Some people feel with women they have to have a bit more of an open-door policy because there may be a few more things that women would talk about, and that they might need some support there. And to some extent that's understandable, but I don't think it requires any more overcompensation than a man. I should have the same privileges talking to my superiors as a man should. They shouldn't be asking me more how are things going, because that kind of centres women out and it makes them feel a little bit more uncomfortable...

Interestingly, some of the leaders stated that they did not feel that military culture needed to change in any major way in order to accommodate women, and in particular did not need to go "overboard". Similarly, another leader felt that although the military, along with society, must change in progressive ways to accommodate women, definitions of effective military leadership need not change in order to accommodate women. The leader quoted below also felt that leadership styles and behaviours need not change with the inclusion of women, but that leadership has already changed in order to adjust to the higher level of education among soldiers compared to the past:

I don't think [leadership needs to change with the inclusion of women in the combat arms]. I think leadership already has gone through a fairly major transformation in combat arms units, from what was once acceptable... You can't just...give the order. ... The soldiers coming in these days are a lot more educated.

The leader quoted above who had been warned against over-accommodating women, further expressed the belief that both women and the military should accommodate each other to a certain extent, with the limit on change being set by the need to maintain operational effectiveness. Similar thoughts were expressed by the leader quoted below, who described masculine and feminine cultures in her troop as existing side by side, even meshing, and reflecting mutual respect. Overall, according to her, the cultural shifts have been small:

> The two cultures in my small experience are going side by side. And it hasn't been radical change, just small shifts… There's been a bit of give and take. I don't get offended when the guys that go "I have to go pee" or whatever, and just turns around. … I haven't come in and been like, oh you can't have that, and you can't do this and you can't do that. So on my level anyway it looks like the two are meshing. … And there's respect for each other and things like that.

When asked whether women should accommodate to military culture, or whether military culture should accommodate to women, one leader said that both should accommodate, but also emphasized the importance of the military "not making a big deal about" the inclusion of women. Indeed, this theme, about not drawing attention to women, or not singling women out, was prevalent in this study. The leader quoted below also expressed the view that change must occur in both women and the military, and that in particular the first group of women in the combat arms would need to accommodate, or assimilate, to the existing military culture, but that over time, the military culture would also change to accommodate women:

> I think the first women do have to do some assimilating, and like everybody in the army has to assimilate to a certain degree because they're adopting certain values, they're adopting a way of life, doing all of that stuff. And maybe to a greater extent the first group of women has to do a little more of that but then as the system grows and changes, it will embrace them more fully and allow them to use their strengths to their greatest potential and will develop their weaknesses. I think that that will happen.

One of the ways in which military culture seems to have changed somewhat, for example, concerns language. The leader quoted below described how she changed some of her superior officers' use of language to make it more gender-neutral or inclusive:

> I know initially when I go into a room I'll be the only woman and somebody would say lady and gentlemen. … I hated that. I hated it because I felt it drew attention to me and I didn't want that. All I wanted to do was to disappear. But now I correct people. … I will always do it privately, but if we continue to use male language always, as silly as it sounds…I respond better to direction when I'm included in a language that I'm being directed in, and I said this to our commanding officer who was very receptive. He would come in and he'd say, gentlemen, orders. And I'd just be like, it's not for me. I'm not included in that. And so he now says, ladies and gentlemen, orders, and I think it's better. Or just orders. … I always refer to my troops, or the men and women I command, because we live in a society that says inclusive language is important, so why is it not true in the Army?

Thus, overall, the women leaders in this study felt that the inclusion of women in the combat arms has changed the military, and military culture, to some extent, for example, by accommodating women's physical needs and embracing certain feminine leadership qualities. Still, the majority of the women in this study felt that change in the military has not, and need not, be radical, and that it must be two-way: in other words, that women must accommodate to the military and the military must accommodate to women. Overall, the women in this study also felt that the military in general, and the combat arms in specific, has come a long way in terms of integrating women in the last few years. In the final part of this chapter, we examine how leaders in the CF, and the CF as an organization, may further enhance gender integration through policies and practices.

Positive Leadership Practices for Enhancing Gender Integration

One of the issues explored in this study concerned the perceptions of participants regarding the role of the leader, or of *positive leadership behaviours*, in facilitating gender integration. All eight leaders indicated that they believed that the leader plays an important role in facilitating gender integration. Some were quite emphatic in stating this view, such as the leader quoted below:

> …If the leader is 100% for the mission, in this case, gender integration, then the troops will say all right, this is definitely something I should be looking at…

In terms of positive leadership behaviours for facilitating gender integration, the three leadership behaviours mentioned the most frequently were having a positive attitude towards women in combat roles (mentioned by all eight leaders): setting an example (mentioned by six of eight leaders); and not singling women out (mentioned by five of eight leaders). The importance of a leader having a *positive attitude regarding women in the combat arms*, was expressed by a leader in the following excerpt:

> My commanding officer is one of the most fantastic commanding officers I've ever had the opportunity to work for, and he is absolutely fair. He sets a high standard of leadership and behaviour, and he doesn't really give one hoot whether people are men or women.

The leader quoted below emphasized the importance of a leader *not singling women out*:

> … just treat them as you would any soldier. Because soldiers are all different, because the men are not all cookie cutter, they're not the same men. Some are strong and some are weak and some are articulate and some are not and some are emotional and some are not. But just…develop that person according to their own individual potential.

Significantly, four leaders mentioned *accepting alternative styles of leadership* as a positive leadership behaviour that would enhance gender integration. For example,

My boss gave me the impression that I had to be much more aggressive and that was the whole point of his feedback. He said that I was too calm and seemed uncertain. And I definitely was uncertain. … But as for the big aggressive part, I said that is not ever going to come out in me. Like, that's not my leadership style. … I mean if I'm yelling or if I'm, then I'm mad, like there is something really wrong. And someone better be dying, or there is something serious going on if... And I don't think that's a bad thing. [Getting that feedback from my superior] was very…that's a highlight in my career, but it's not a good highlight.

Three leaders, such as the one quoted below, mentioned *refraining from gender stereotyping and from using sexist humour or sexist language* as another positive leadership behaviour:

And there's things that every leader can do that are not simply true for gender integration but are true…right across the board. For one, never, never ever tolerate…sexist language. … Now, that doesn't mean that…if someone's telling a joke that's a funny joke that perhaps has sexual connotations, that's fine, but truly sexist language or sexist ideas, we can't tolerate, especially as a woman, I can't allow that kind of thing to go on. But by the same token, any kind of racist language, which is something that we deal with now, any kind of religious, anti-religious, certainly none of those things. That's something that's very important at the leadership level, to stomp that kind of stuff out before it starts.

Possessing *basic leadership competence* was also mentioned as a positive leadership behaviour by three leaders. These leadership competencies included, for example, being able to deal with fraternization issues, sexual harassment, and gender-related logistical issues.

As far as the sexual thing [fraternization] is concerned, that I believe is just an extremely archaic argument because they said the same thing about women coming into the medical profession, they said the same thing about women as leaders in large organizations previously male, and it's worked out fine. I mean all it takes is common sense and it takes discretion…on the part of the leadership and perhaps a little bit of sensitivity on the side of the leadership to take a look at situations and say no, we want to avoid this one, we want to develop this one. So that is just a problem that we have in life and sure, if you want to hide from the reality of society, you can, but I don't think that the benefits that bringing women in, [that women] bring to the CF, certainly that does not outweigh the benefits that can be gained.

The setting of *gender-free performance standards* was also mentioned by two leaders as a positive leadership behaviour. (Note that the excerpt below also illustrates the importance of not singling women out.)

Not to allow double standards. That's something that is as important as, developing, like one of the things we have to do is develop every soldier, whether it's a man or a woman, where they are weak, and praise them where they are strong and if, say for example, one of my soldiers is physically weak and it happens to be a woman, then it is my job to help develop her physically, and that's what I mean by [not] allowing double standards. … So I think that's really important is to hold them to that physical standard…to hold them to it and not say, oh they can't.

Not defining gender integration issues as simply a woman's problem was seen as another positive leadership behaviour (mentioned by two leaders). For example, one participant argued that every individual in a leadership role, not just women, should be knowledgeable enough about women's kit and equipment to ensure that everyone in their unit has an optimum fit and is, therefore, properly equipped to do the job. Other positive leadership behaviours, mentioned less often by participants, involved the importance of *communicating with followers* (mentioned by one leader quoted below):

Now, I don't think there's anything wrong with when a [commander] sits down and has his interview with the one or the two women who are in his [unit] to say, listen, you could experience things like this, we've seen something like this in the past. If it happens, let me know. It's unacceptable. Like, that kind of thing, just simplify it and allow them to use the chain of command.

Despite the fact that most participants spoke of the importance of leaders not singling out women, another positive leadership behaviour involved the importance of *acknowledging and dealing with gender differences*, such as gender differences in learning styles, as mentioned by one leader quoted below:

[As a leader] you just have to figure out how people learn something, men or women, and…if they learn different, teach them different.

Finally, the ability to *understand family issues* was also seen as a positive leadership behaviour, which was mentioned by one leader quoted below:

I made the conscious decision [that due to family circumstances] I did not want to go away for two months…and so I talked to the CO [who suggested I look after the rear party]. … So I looked after rear party. … So I mean, and it worked out well.

In summary, the women leaders in this study expressed the view that the leader does in fact play an important role in facilitating gender integration. The women spoke of a number of positive leadership behaviours that could enhance gender integration, including: expressing positive attitudes regarding women in combat; setting the example; not singling women out; accepting alternative leadership styles; refraining from gender stereotyping or the use of sexist humour/sexist language; demonstrating basic leadership competence; setting gender-neutral performance standards; not defining gender integration issues as simply a woman's problem; communicating with followers; acknowledging and dealing with gender differences; and understanding family issues.[35]

Canadian Forces Organizational Policies and Practices for Enhancing Gender Integration

The women in this study were also asked about what the CF could do, as an organization, to enhance gender integration. Similar to the themes that emerged regarding positive leadership practices, one of the key themes that emerged regarding the CF as an organization was the importance of not singling women out, and of treating everyone with uniformity and fairness. Some leaders felt that a mentoring program would be helpful for integrating women into the CF. The leader quoted below, for instance, felt that a mentoring program would be beneficial in terms of women's career development, but she also cautioned about potential adverse effects (i.e., singling out women in a mentoring program):

> I think mentoring would probably be a great thing for women. But it would, I suspect, be received poorly as…putting women in a position of privilege, empowering them as a group and identifying them as a group, which you'd have to lay out whether the benefits would be more than the drawbacks…[because it might be another form of singling out].

The leader quoted below felt that while a formal mentoring program may not be necessary, mentoring, and in particular, successful women role models, could help inspire women in the combat arms:

> I don't know that it needs to be something formal, but it's always nice to see someone who is even just slightly ahead of you in their career progression who has encountered, and to say, she did it, so I can, too. … I think as we get more and more women in to the key positions or higher ranks that we will see more and more. [They can act as role models more than] mentors.

In contrast, the leader quoted below felt that a formal mentoring program, particularly one that matched new female recruits with more experienced women was not a good idea, for she felt that a woman could learn as much from a man as from a woman:

A mentoring program where the females were matched with females [would not be a good idea]. You can learn as much from a man as you can a woman. ... All you need is someone that's supportive and is willing to help you out. But I think a mentoring thing is better left informal. ... I think that kind of program would be a complete waste of money and time.

Interestingly, many of the women in this study expressed criticisms of the CF's former Standard for Harassment and Racism Prevention (SHARP) training program (a gender/diversity awareness course). The leader quoted below felt that such programs are a complete waste of time:

Well again, we're all SHARP trained which is X's and O's but it caused more jokes afterwards than it did before, so I think that was a complete waste of time. But no, diversity training would be a huge waste of money because...making a spectacle and saying this guy is Asian, you can't bother him or she's female, you can't bother her. Well, I think everyone knows that by now. So it's a huge waste of time.

The leader quoted below felt that although SHARP was a good program in theory, in practice, it was divisive. She also, however, suggested an alternative approach for making diversity programs more effective (i.e., by integrating them into basic-level training as "teamwork" or "leadership" courses, rather than "gender awareness" courses):

[SHARP training or other gender awareness or diversity training courses are] not a good thing. .... They're great in concept but in delivery I do not think it's possible to deliver them and get the intended result. They come across to our soldiers and our officers as being political, and they come across as being stereotypical and divisive. ... [Instead], focus on the training system. ...Make it part of lectures and make it subtle. ... It should be taught as teamwork, it should be taught at the basic level...and...it shouldn't be identified as a gender topic, it should be identified as a leadership and teamwork and morale/cohesion problem.

In contrast, the leader quoted below felt that SHARP training and similar programs were useful and, if implemented appropriately, need not single anyone out:

> ...Some form of that kind of program I think does have to be there, especially for newer recruits getting in who have to understand the Canadian Forces policy on gender integration and harassment and those types of things. ... I think it's a useful thing and...if it's done appropriately, I don't think it centres anybody out.

Another participant indicated that, while imperfect, both the SHARP training and the CF harassment policy were needed to ensure that senior leaders know what they are doing wrong and that everyone gains a basic level of awareness.

Some participants spoke about the need to have gender-neutral, but job-related fitness standards for women and men, in order to dispel any perceptions of unequal treatment:

> There is a fitness standard that is accepted for women and one that is accepted for men. And I understand the principle behind that, because we are physically different... ... [But] I think that there should be one standard, and if it has to be lowered to bring women in, well then that standard still has to be able to allow me to do my job. ... I think if we had that one standard, that would get rid of a lot of the concerns because then the men when they go through, well, she met the same standard as us so you can't criticize her physical shape because you just achieved the same standard.

On the other hand, the participant quoted below agreed that whereas gender-specific fitness standards made sense, occupation-specific standards should be gender-neutral (as is the case in the CF), in order to increase the likelihood that women will be accepted:

> There's a reason to have a male and a female fitness standard... because some jobs are very different from other jobs and there is a

recognized physical difference between men and women. But for trade specific, [the same standard for women and men] I think is very important.

At least one participant warned against the use of a quota system to increase the representation of women in the combat arms. Her resistance to such a system was based on her experience with a previous application of a quota system that she believed created a stigma for women, that still exists, in the regiment.[36] The participant quoted below felt that the CF should not try to push women into the combat arms in order to increase their representation, but that it should let women integrate "naturally" and not "over-accommodate" women (e.g., in terms of special fitness standards):

> I think it's a process that's just going to have to happen slowly and gradually regardless of timelines that they have and standards they have to meet and whatnot. They can't force it, and they're trying to force it and then everyone's like, ooh, look at this, you know.

On the other hand, some of the leaders, such as the one quoted below, felt that the CF could facilitate gender integration by addressing some of the "little things," like having female-designated showers, or supplying women with equipment that fits properly. Quite simply stated by one participant "Get us the equipment to do our job". The leader quoted below expressed a similar sentiment regarding the need for equipment suitable to women:

> If they had the right equipment, it would probably be ten times easier. Like a ruck-sack that fits the back of a woman, webbing that doesn't get caught on your breasts, boots that fit a feminine foot, clothing that just works…

Nevertheless, the women leaders in this study generally felt that, overall, the CF was doing what it could do to promote gender integration, that doing any more would be "pushing things," and that, overall, the CF has made great strides in gender integration and recruiting practices. Forcing the issue any further, according to at least one woman, would make it "more difficult for the women that are already in…by getting the wrong people in the jobs".

In summary, the women leaders in this study identified a number of CF organizational policies and practices that could enhance gender integration. In particular, they emphasized the importance of not singling women out, of adopting gender-neutral standards (especially occupational standards), of allowing gender integration to occur more "naturally" as opposed to pushing or over-accommodating women, and of providing suitable equipment/kit for women. Some women also spoke in favour of mentoring programs and role models, but some cautioned against having formal mentoring programs, as they felt that these could unduly single women out. Similarly, some of the women thought that gender awareness programs were a good idea in theory, but emphasized the importance of implementing such programs properly, while others thought that such programs were a "waste of time." Overall, most of the women leaders in this study felt that the CF was doing all that it could to integrate women effectively in the combat arms, and that the CF had made significant strides in gender integration in recent years.

Discussion

The present chapter sought to address current perspectives and experiences of women leaders in the CF combat arms regarding several issues pertaining to gender and leadership. When asked to reflect generally on their visions of effective leadership, for example, the women leaders in this study spoke of both masculine characteristics (e.g., emotional control) and feminine characteristics (e.g., communication skills) as being important, suggesting that they do not define effective leadership in strictly masculine *or* feminine terms, but see value in possessing both masculine and feminine characteristics that could be applied flexibly to different circumstances. A similar result was obtained recently by Boyce and Herd[37] who found that female cadet leaders perceived successful officers as having characteristics commonly ascribed to both women and men.[38]

Further, in terms of strategies for enhancing their own leadership effectiveness, most leaders in this study did not feel that they must adopt a masculine leadership style in order to be seen as effective; rather, they felt that they could develop their own leadership style and "be themselves." Moreover, perhaps one of the strongest indications of integration is the finding that all eight leaders in this study described their own leadership style in integrative, or even androgynous,[39] terms. Some leaders even seemed to emphasize the importance of their feminine attributes to effective leadership. They mentioned being intuitive; they mentioned the gratification they experienced through developing followers; and they mentioned their interpersonal skills, their approachability, their ability to read and understand others, and their ability to listen. Indeed, this study indicated that women leaders in the combat arms have been adopting alternative styles of leadership – styles that are more feminine (person-oriented, empowering, participative, and democratic) – not to the exclusion of masculine characteristics but in addition to them.[40] Similarly, Korabik and Ayman[41] have argued that to be an effective leader it is important to have both instrumental, or masculine, and interpersonal, or feminine, skills. Task-oriented skills such as independence, decisiveness, and competitiveness are needed to get the job done, whereas person-oriented skills such as warmth, understanding, co-operativeness, and consideration for others are associated with high morale and cohesiveness in the workplace.[42] Several of the leaders in this study also indicated that gender plays a role in defining leadership effectiveness, whether in terms of gender differences in leadership style or qualities, or in terms of gender differences in what it takes to be perceived as an effective leader.

Yet, despite the fact that most participants defined effective leadership at least partly in terms of feminine attributes, some of the women also described negative outcomes (e.g., lack of respect from peers/followers) associated with a female leader exhibiting a feminine leadership style and/or feminine characteristics. These could be considered forms of resistance against women in leadership roles in the combat arms. For instance, participants warned against a female leader adopting feminine roles or having a feminine physical appearance; they warned against a female leader being "sexually provocative" or being seen as a "sexual object;" and they warned against a female leader being too caring or compassionate. Such warnings are reminiscent of the female cadets studied by Yoder[43] who tried to blend in with the men by wearing pants but not skirts.[44] Although some of the women leaders in this study stated that they felt comfortable, for example, wearing whatever clothes they wished (when not in uniform), the more frequently voiced perception was that women had to be careful about their physical appearance at all times. In contrast, and counter to what would be expected from role congruity theory,[45] relatively few participants anticipated any negative implications arising from a female leader exhibiting a masculine leadership style and/or masculine characteristics.[46] Still, this study suggests that a "catch-22" or dilemma (e.g., between being seen as too aggressive vs. too timid) may still be prevalent for women in leadership, and that leadership for women in the combat arms may still be perceived as "a tricky balance."[47]

The women in this study also spoke of various other forms of resistance that they encountered as women leaders in the combat arms, such as difficulties with male peers; gender stereotypes; demands to "act like a boy;" failing courses simply because of their gender; sexual rumours; and sexist jokes. The women challenged these forms of resistance in various ways, for example, by challenging generalizations about women and men's emotional characteristics (and thus, challenging gender stereotypes), and by advocating for gender-neutral physical standards in order to offset concerns about women's physical abilities. Interestingly, several women spoke against the CF treating women "too well" by over-accommodating women (e.g., giving them clerk positions) because this could be perceived as singling women out and ultimately works against women's career advancement. In general, the women voiced many concerns about being singled out, whether by the media or the CF (e.g., to perform certain roles such as gender/diversity advisor). Related to this is another form of resistance that some of the women talked about: that of the greater scrutiny they experienced as minorities in a male-dominated environment.[48] Despite the various forms of resistance that they encountered, however, the women in this study generally spoke very enthusiastically about their jobs and were optimistic that performing well and proving themselves (e.g., physically or in battle) would go a long way towards addressing any resistance to women leaders that may still persist in the CF/combat arms.

The women leaders in this study also felt that the inclusion of women in the combat arms has changed the military and military culture to a certain degree (e.g., by accommodating women's physical needs and embracing certain feminine leadership qualities). They felt that change in military culture need not be radical, however, and that while the military must accommodate women to some extent, women (especially the first groups of women to enter the combat arms) also needed to adapt or assimilate to the military/combat arms. In other words, the views of the women in this study reflected two perspectives on culture change in the case where a minority (women) meets a majority (the male-dominated combat arms): integration and assimilation.[49] According to Berry,[50] assimilation emphasizes similarity and implies a relinquishing of minority group identity and a move towards the dominant group culture. In integration, both the majority and the minority orientations are equally valued, and both similarities and differences between the minority and the majority groups are recognized and respected.[51] Further, within integration, aspects of the cultural integrity of a minority group are maintained (i.e., there is some resistance to acculturation), but there is also some movement towards becoming an integral part of the larger framework (i.e., there is some adjustment).[52] According to Korabik,[53] in integration, the minority group changes, but the minority group also influences the majority group and the existing system to change.[54]

In this study, the women felt that the military in general, and the combat arms in specific, has come a long way in terms of integrating women in the last few years. And indeed, there is evidence that some form of cultural integration has occurred in the combat arms. For example, when speaking in general terms about leadership effectiveness, the majority of women in this study saw value in both masculine and feminine leadership characteristics; that is, they spoke of effective leadership in androgynous terms, as drawing on or integrating both masculine and feminine characteristics. Furthermore, most of the leaders in this study did not feel that they must adopt a masculine style in order to be perceived as effective. Perhaps one of the strongest indications of integration is the finding that all eight of the leaders in this study described feminine attributes as important aspects of their own leadership style. However, there is also considerable evidence that cultural assimilation, from a gender perspective, is still prevalent in the CF combat arms. One piece of evidence concerns the negative implications that participants perceived in relation to female leaders adopting feminine styles of leadership (or feminine characteristics exhibited by female leaders).

The women in this study also suggested a number of positive leadership behaviours and CF organizational policies and practices that could serve to further enhance gender integration. Positive leadership practices included: expressing positive attitudes regarding women in combat roles; setting the example; not singling women out; accepting alternative leadership styles; refraining from gender stereotyping or the use of sexist humour/sexist language; demonstrating basic leadership competence; setting gender-neutral performance standards; not defining gender integration issues as simply a woman's problem; communicating with followers; acknowledging and dealing with gender differences; and understanding family issues. Similarly, CF organizational policies and practices for enhancing gender integration included: not singling women out; adopting gender-neutral standards (especially occupational standards); allowing gender integration to occur more "naturally" as opposed to "over-accommodating" women; and providing suitable equipment/kit for women, role models, mentoring programs (particularly informal programs); and gender awareness programs (if implemented properly). Once again, most of the women leaders in this study felt that, although challenges remain, the CF was doing all that it could to integrate women effectively in the combat arms, and that the CF had made significant strides in gender integration in recent years.

In focusing on women leaders in the combat arms, this study allowed for a more current understanding of women's perspectives, and perceptions, regarding leadership and gender integration. However, future research should also explore the perspectives and experiences of other women in the combat arms (e.g., at other army bases across Canada), other military women (including women in the Air Force and Navy), and military women who have served in operational (particularly war-fighting) environments. Such studies may contribute to a better understanding of military culture in the CF and the process of its change.

ENDNOTES

1   The one exclusion to the court order, submarine service, was removed in March, 2001.

2   N.J. Holden & L.M. Tanner, *An examination of current gender integration policies in TTCP countries*. Director Strategic Human Resource Coordination Personnel Operational Research Team & Director Military Gender Integration and Employment Equity ORD Report R2001/01 (Ottawa, Canada: Department of National Defence, 2001). According to figures released by the Director Military Gender Integration and Employment Equity (DMGIEE) in 2003, women account, overall, for 14.1% of CF officers and 11.9% of non-commissioned members (NCMs); overall, 12.4% of CF members were women. However, there are inter-service differences. For example, according to the 2001 CF Self-identification Census report, women represented 19% of the Air Force, 17.9% of the Navy, and only 12.6% of the Army (N. J. Holden, *The Canadian Forces 2001 Self-Identification Census: Methodology and Preliminary Results.* D Strat HR Research Note RN 01/03 (Ottawa, Canada: Department of National Defence, Director Military Gender Integration and Employment Equity & Director Strategic Human Resources, 2003). In 2003, the Committee on Women in NATO forces indicated that women comprise 16.6% of the Air Force (14.8% of officers and 17.3% of NCMs); 11.5% of the Navy (15.9% of officers and 10.2% of NCMs); and 9.6% of the Army (11.8% of officers and 9.2% of NCMs).

3   L. Tanner, *Gender Integration in the Canadian Forces: A Quantitative and Qualitative Analysis.* Director General Military Human Resources Policy & Planning, Directorate of Military Gender Integration & Employment Equity, & Director General Operational Research Directorate of Operational Research (Corporate, Air & Maritime), ORD Report R9901. (Ottawa, Canada: Department of National Defence, 1999).

4   See, for example, J. Boldry, W. Wood, & D.A. Kashy, "Gender stereotypes and the evaluation of men and women in military training" *Journal of Social Issues*, 57(4, 2001), 689-705; A.H. Eagly, S.J. Karau, & M.G. Makhijani, M. G., *Psychological Bulletin*, 117 (1995), 125-145; and, R.W. Rice, J.D. Yoder, J. Adams, R.F. Priest, & H.T. Prince, H. T., "Leadership ratings for male and female military cadets" *Sex Roles*, 10 (11/12, 1984), 885-901.

5   See, for example, A.H. Eagly, M.C. Johannesen-Schmidt, & M.L. van Engen, M. L., "Transformational, transactional, and laissez-faire leadership styles: A meta-analysis comparing women and men" *Psychological Bulletin*, 129(4, 2003), 569-591; A.H. Eagly, & B.T. Johnson, "Gender and leadership style: A meta-analysis" *Psychological Bulletin*, 108 (1990), 233-256; Eagly, Karau, & Makhijani, "Gender and

the effectiveness of leaders: A meta-analysis"; and R. P. Vecchio, "Leadership and gender advantage" *The Leadership Quarterly*, 13 (2002), 643-671.

6   V. O'Leary, "Some attitudinal barriers to occupational aspirations in women" *Psychological Bulletin*, 81 (1974), 809-826; V.E. Schein, "The relationship between sex-role stereotypes and requisite management characteristics" *Journal of Applied Psychology*, 57 (1973), 95-100; and V.E. Schein, "The relationship between sex-role stereotypes and requisite management characteristics among female managers" *Journal of Applied Psychology*, 60 (1975), 340-344.

7   L.A. Boyce & A.M. Herd, "The relationship between gender role stereotypes and requisite military leadership characteristics" *Sex Roles*, 49 (7/8, 2003), 365-378.

8   Ibid.

9   S.A. Hill, *Identification of women's leadership in the Canadian Forces.* (Kingston, ON: Canadian Forces Leadership Institute, 2001).

10   Eagly, Karau, & Makhijani, "Gender and the effectiveness of leaders: A meta-analysis".

11   Boldry, Wood, & Kashy, "Gender stereotypes and the evaluation of men and women in military training".

12   See also J. Adams, J. (1984). "Women at West Point: A three-year perspective." *Sex Roles*, 11(5/6, 1984), 525-541; and R.W. Rice, J.D. Yoder, J. Adams, R.F. Priest, & H.T. Prince, H. T., "Leadership ratings for male and female military cadets" Adams, 1984; and Rice, Yoder, Adams, Priest, & Prince, 1984).

13   Eagly, Karau, and Makhijani, "Gender and the effectiveness of leaders: A meta-analysis".

14   Eagly & Johnson, "Gender and leadership style: A meta-analysis".

15   Boldry, Wood, & Kashy, "Gender stereotypes and the evaluation of men and women in military training"; and R.W. Rice, D. Instone, D & J. Adams, "Leader sex, leader success, and leadership process: Two field studies" *Journal of Applied Psychology*, 69 (1, 1984), 12-31.

16   e.g., K.D. Davis, & V. Thomas, *Chief land staff gender integration study: The experience of women who have served in the combat arms.* (Personnel Research Team Sponsor Research Report 98-1). Ottawa, Canada: National Defence Headquarters, 1998.

17   Ibid.

18 K.D. Davis, *Chief land staff gender integration study: The regular force training and employment environment.* (Personnel Research Team Sponsor Research Report 97-2). Ottawa, Canada: National Defence Headquarters, 1997.

19 Ibid.

20 Ibid.

21 Ibid.

22 J.D. Yoder, *Women and gender: Transforming psychology.* (Upper Saddle River, NJ: Prentice-Hall, 1999).

23 Ibid.

24 Ibid.

25 Ibid.

26 Davis & Thomas, *Chief land staff gender integration study: The experience of women who have served in the combat arms.*

27 Yoder, *Women and gender: Transforming psychology.*

28 This group of 26 women represented 83.9% of the total number of women in combat arms occupations at CFB Petawawa (31) at the time the study was conducted in 2003 (see A.R. Febbraro, *Women, leadership and gender integration in the Canadian combat arms: A qualitative study.* DRDC Toronto TR 2003-170. Defence Research and Development Canada – Toronto, 2003).

29 E.G. Guba, "Criteria for assessing the trustworthiness of naturalistic inquiries" *Educational Communication and Technology Journal*, 29 (2, 1981), 75-91.

30 E.g., R.F. Bales, *Interaction process analysis: A method for the study of small groups* (Reading, MA: Addison-Wesley, 1950; S.L. Bem, "The measurement of psychological androgyny" *Journal of Consulting and Clinical Psychology*, 42 (1974), 155-162; L.A. Boyce & A.M. Herd, "The relationship between gender role stereotypes and requisite military leadership characteristics"; I.K. Broverman, D.M. Broverman, F.E. Clarkson, P. Rosenkrantz, & S.R. Vogel, "Sex-role stereotypes and clinical judgments of mental health" *Journal of Consulting and Clinical Psychology*, 34 (1970), 1-7; I.K. Broverman, S.R. Vogel, D.M. Broverman, F.E. Clarkson, & P.S. Rosenkrantz, P. S. "Sex-role stereotypes: A current appraisal" *Journal of Social Issues*, 28 (1972), 59-78; and A.H. Eagly, M.G. Makhijani, & B.G. Klonsky, "Gender and the evaluation of leaders: A meta-analysis" *Psychological Bulletin*, 111 (1992), 3-22.

31 M.Q. Patton, *Qualitative evaluation methods.* (Beverly Hills, CA: Sage, 1980).

32 Although the interviews were transcribed verbatim, the interview excerpts that are presented in this chapter have been edited slightly to enhance their readability.

33 In addition, the women leaders also spoke about gender-neutral aspects of effective leadership, such as being consistent; being perceptive; having a sense of humour; being able to lead a diverse, well educated army; and being flexible and adaptable (see A.R. Febbraro, *Women, leadership and gender integration in the Canadian combat arms: A qualitative study*).

34 In contrast, only one of the eight leaders described negative outcomes associated with a female leader adopting a masculine leadership style (see Febbraro, *Women, leadership and gender integration in the Canadian combat arms: A qualitative study*).

35 In the larger study which included followers, two additional positive leadership behaviour for enhancing gender integration were mentioned: mentoring, and inspiring teamwork between women and men soldiers (see A.R. Febbraro, *Women, leadership and gender integration in the Canadian combat arms: A qualitative study*).

36 Despite common misperceptions, quota systems have never been used to increase the representation of women and other designated groups (visible minorities, Aboriginal Peoples, persons with disabilities) in the CF, as the conditions of the Employment Equity Act prohibit the establishment of quotas. The CF has established a long-term (20-year) recruitment goal of 28% for women (25% for the Army), but this is not the same as a quota system.

37 Boyce & Herd, "The relationship between gender role stereotypes and requisite military leadership characteristics"

38 See also A.H. Eagly, M.C. Johannesen-Schmidt, & M.L. van Engen, M. L., "Transformational, transactional, and laissez-faire leadership styles: A meta-analysis comparing women and men"; and J.D. Yoder, "Another look at women in the United States Army: A comment on Woelfel's article".

39 S.L. Bem, "The measurement of psychological androgyny".

40 F.L. Denmark, "Women, leadership, and empowerment" *Psychology of Women Quarterly*, 17 (1993), 343-356.

41 Similarly, K. Korabik & R. Ayman, "Do women managers have to act like men?: *Journal of Management Development*, 8 (6, 1989), 23-32.

42 Ibid.

43 J.D. Yoder, *Women and gender: Transforming psychology*.

44 See also J. Marshall, "Organizational cultures and women managers: Exploring the dynamics of resilience" *Applied Psychology: An International Review*, 42 (4, 1993), 313-322.

45 Eagly, Karau, & Makhijani, "Gender and the effectiveness of leaders: A meta-analysis".

46 In the larger study that included followers (see A.R. Febbraro, *Women, leadership and gender integration in the Canadian combat arms: A qualitative study*; and A.R. Febbraro, "Gender and leadership in the Canadian Forces combat arms: A qualitative study of assimilation vs. integration" *The Canadian Journal of Police & Security Services*, 2 (4, 2004), 215-228) one-half of the followers felt that women leaders must become more masculine in order to be seen as effective. This finding is in marked contrast to the finding for leaders, nearly all of whom felt that they could be themselves and still be considered effective leaders, and that they did not have to assimilate to a masculine leadership model. For many followers, it seems that "fitting in with the guys" and being part of the group is of paramount importance. Apart from differences in officer-NCM status, possible explanations for this difference between followers and leaders may be due to differences in educational background, specific command/leadership experiences, courses and training, age/maturity, or other factors.

47 For an account of a similar catch-22 described by army women in the CF land trial in the 1980s, in which women felt "damned if you do and damned if you don't take on masculine attributes, see L.M. Phillipo, *Content analysis of land trial interviews 1980 and 1983*. (Technical Note 17/84). (Willowdale, Ontario: Canadian Forces Personnel Applied Research Unit, 1984).

48 R.M. Kanter, *Men and women of the corporation*. (New York: Basic Books, 1977).

49 J.W. Berry, "Acculturation and psychological adaptation" p. 511-520 in J. Forgas & J. Innes (Eds.), Recent advances in social psychology: *An international perspective* (Amsterdam: Elsevier, 1989).

50 Ibid.

51 Korabik, 1993.

52 J.W. Berry, "Acculturation: A comparative analysis of alternative forms" pp. 66-77 in R.J. Samuda & A.L. Woods (Eds.), *Perspectives in immigrant and minority education* (Lanham, MD: University Press of America, 1983); and J.W. Berry, "Acculturation and psychological adaptation".

53   K. Korabik, *Strangers in a strange land: Women managers and the legitimization of authority.* Paper presented as part of the symposium entitled "The Legitimization of Women's Authority" at the annual meeting of the Canadian Psychological Association, Montreal, Quebec, Canada (May 1993).

54   see also C. Lamerson, *Integration of women into previously all-male units: A literature review.* (Working Paper 87-2). (Willowdale, Ontario: Canadian Forces Personnel Applied Research Unit, 1987) and ; and P.W. Remmington, P. W. (1983). "Women in the police: Integration or separation?" *Qualitative Sociology,* 6 (2, 1983), 118-135.

CHAPTER 9

Leadership and Women: Should We Be Leading 'Like a Man' or Adopting Women's Ways?

Lieutenant-Commander Lynn Bradley

Women have been given advice on *How to succeed in business without being one of the boys*[1] and been told that progress towards gender equality has invariably been met with substantial backlash.[2] They have been informed that when it comes to leadership, there is a female advantage[3] and have been encouraged to look *Beyond the double bind*[4] of concurrently trying to maintain both gender appropriateness and leadership effectiveness. Women have been advised to "act and dress more like a manager and less like a secretary".[5] They have been described as iron maidens,[6] as *Strangers in a strange land*,[7] as honorary men,[8] and as agents of change.[9] Clearly, whether they turn to the popular narratives or to the academic literature, those who are interested in women and leadership, or women who aspire to be leaders, have been bombarded with conflicting information, advice, and admonishments.

This chapter discusses the state of the art and science regarding women and leadership. It first establishes the context by briefly describing leadership research generally, followed by the more specific and current exploration of research themes in the women and leadership literature. It then examines alternative perspectives with an emphasis on the continuing social construction of gender and leadership in organizations. A response to the question 'Should we be leading like a man or adopting women's ways of leading?' is provided, as are suggestions for further research.

An Overview of Leadership Research

It has been said that leadership is the most extensively researched organizational psychology construct. *Bass and Stogdill's Handbook*[10] includes over 5,000 references related to leadership issues. Definitions for this construct are abundant.[11] For example, Stogdill defined leadership as "the process (act) of influencing the activities of an organized group in its efforts toward goal setting and goal achievement",[12] which was subsequently expanded by including consideration for the well-being and feelings of group members.[13] There is generally some agreement across definitions that leadership involves interacting with other people in pursuit of a common goal. Inherent in the leader, as opposed to the follower, is the notion of influencing or persuading others to set aside individual desires or goals in order to pursue a goal important to the group.[14,*]

Hersey and Blanchard expanded the basic definition by considering leadership to be "the process of influencing the activities of an individual or a group in efforts toward goal achievement in a *given situation*"[15] (emphasis added). Contingency approaches considered leadership to be a product of leader characteristics and the situation, the latter including relationships between leader and followers.[16] Leadership was thus viewed as a process that encompasses the leader and the follower, as well as the situation.

These three basic components of leadership are reflected in the main approaches to the study of this construct. Although some researchers have investigated particular constructs such as need for power or achievement,[17] generally leadership theories can be classified as trait, behavioural, or situational, or some combination of these approaches. More recently, leadership research has focused on relational-based theories.[18]

Trait theories of leadership[19] attempted to specify the personality, abilities, and other attributes of leaders that are primary influences on effectiveness. In addition to intelligence, certain personality traits have been found to predict managerial effectiveness. Barrick and Mount[20] found that, of the so-called Big

---

*   Canadian Forces Leadership doctrine defines leadership as "directly or indirectly influencing others, by means of formal authority or personal attributes, to act in accordance with one's intent or a shared purpose." National Defence, *Leadership in the Canadian Forces: Doctrine.* (Canadian Defence Academy – Canadian Forces Leadership Institute, 2005), 3.

Five personality traits,[21] extraversion and conscientiousness were most strongly related to managerial effectiveness while Tett, Jackson, and Rothstein[22] found that all five of these traits (emotional stability, agreeableness, and openness to experience, in addition to extraversion and conscientiousness) were related to managerial effectiveness. The trait approach is typified by the notion that leaders are born and not made.

Behavioural approaches are based on the concept that leader effectiveness differs depending on the particular behaviours exhibited in performing the role of leader. A major implication of this approach is that one could be trained to be a leader. To be a leader, one merely has to adopt the appropriate leader behaviours, which can be learned. Which behaviours are crucial differs depending on the theoretical approach taken. Task-relevant behaviour, which is aimed at accomplishing the tasks or goals assigned to the group, and person-relevant behaviour, which includes activities that foster positive group interactions, are dimensions typically considered. Theories in line with a behavioural approach include those outlined by the Ohio State studies of leadership,[23] which considered two fundamental dimensions of leadership, *initiating structure* and *consideration*, and the Blake and Mouton[24] grid approach, which described leaders based on their preferred behaviours and position in a nine-point grid along the dimensions of *employee-oriented* and *task-oriented* behaviours.

Situational theories of leadership[25] provided models outlining the most appropriate leader behaviours for a given situation. These approaches focused on the behaviours of leaders and their effects on followers. Crucial leader skills included diagnosing the situation in order to determine the most appropriate leadership behaviours and adapting leadership style to that situation.[26] Stogdill noted that the situational approach "denied the influences of individual differences, attributing all variance between persons to fortuitous demands of the environment".[27] He found that leaders and non-leaders did indeed exhibit different personality traits, although situational factors also played a key role. Stogdill[28] and Yukl[29] considered that leadership is influenced by both individual differences and situational variables and both insisted that this view was not a return to the trait-based view that leaders are born. Leadership theories that focus on day-to-day interactions, rewards, and incremental changes in follower behaviours have been termed *transactional* theories (e.g., Ohio State studies, Leader-member exchange theory).

More recently, researchers have been investigating leadership as a process and focusing to a larger extent on the follower or issues relating to interactions with followers. Examples of relational-based theories include *values leadership*, which focused on fostering a climate which nourishes values of excellence, justice, and learning,[30] *enabling leadership*, which emphasized the contribution of all group members in a manner whereby group leadership passes from one person to another as the situation dictated,[31] and *transformational leadership*.[32]

Transformational leadership seeks to heighten the awareness of followers, colleagues, and others about the issues of consequence and build, or indeed inspire, commitment to major changes in organizational initiatives. Pawar and Eastman[33] suggested that this may be accomplished through a vision that changes cultural values and bonds individual and collective interests. Transformational leadership is seen as a sort of higher order extension of transactional leadership that is more intense and powerful for both leader and followers and which results in *Leadership and performance beyond expectations*, the title of Bass's book on the topic.[34]

Leadership in general, then, is regarded as some form of an interaction of leader, follower, and situational variables. Traits, in addition to being useful in the selection of leaders or managers, may also be useful in assessing a predisposition to engage in behaviours or to actively employ appropriate strategies or skills. Behavioural theories further address skills and strategies and the situational context is also important for effective leadership. Each of these main approaches can be identified in the literature that has examined women, or more often gender differences, and leadership.

Women and Leadership

The model of the successful manager in our culture is a masculine one. The good manager is aggressive, competitive, firm and just. He is not feminine, he is not soft and yielding or dependent or intuitive in the womanly sense. The very expression of emotion is widely viewed as a feminine weakness that would interfere with effective business processes.[35]

Despite an impressive history of research on leadership spanning more than half a century, it was only in the 1970s with increasing numbers of women in the workplace and a rise in human rights and equality, that women and leadership became the topic of academic research. Not surprisingly, given that women's employment had been largely segregated into domestic and other generally subservient jobs,[36] initial findings were that leadership was an attribute of men but not of women. There was a great deal of commonality between the stereotype of leader and the stereotype of man, but women were viewed as substantially different. For example, in separate studies,[37] men and women middle managers rated women, men, and successful managers on 92 descriptive terms. As hypothesized, for both men and women, successful managers were perceived to have the characteristics, temperaments, and attitudes most usually ascribed to men. The results of a replication in the late 1980s[38] indicated that, while women indicated resemblance between *woman* and *manager*, ratings by men were essentially unchanged.

As is evident in McGregor's[39] description of *The professional manager* above, the male traits associated with leadership were also generally more positive attributes (e.g., strong, powerful, decisive, assertive) than the rather weak traits associated with women (e.g., emotional, timid, nurturing). As Halford and Leonard[40] noted, "women are perceived as being merely the embodiment of a cluster of 'feminine' attributes rather than suitable management material". O'Leary[41] considered that attitudes of the day towards women managers resulted from the cultural norm that women should not have authority over men. This view is clearly consistent with some of the trait adjectives typically ascribed to men, such as dominant, authoritative, and forceful.

The person-oriented and task-oriented dichotomy[42] and the similar bifurcation of consideration and initiating structure[43] of the behavioural approaches to leadership came to be viewed as rough analogues of women's and men's ways of leading (or managing).[44] That is, typically women's leadership styles were considered to focus on developing and maintaining relationships, interpersonal communication, and distributed power.[45] Helgeson,[46] for example, used the web of inclusion metaphor to describe women's preferred organizational structure. Men's leadership styles, in contrast, were viewed as task-oriented, uncaring of working relationships except insofar as task accomplishment was necessary, and hierarchical in structure with attendant clear lines of authority and power.[47] Implicit in these categorizations was the pervasive implication that being task-oriented, or concerned about goal accomplishment and getting the job done, was a positive attribute or behaviour in a leader, while being more concerned about people than about meeting organizational goals was correspondingly less positive. This implication could be constructed as a belief that 'women may be nice but men get the job done'.

A liberal feminist perspective on leadership suggests that the gender differences that may exist are due to men and women being differentially socialized with respect to masculinity and femininity and sex role orientation. However, there is a large gap between what are considered men's and women's traits or characteristics and those which men and women possess.[48] Not all men display masculine attributes and not all women possess feminine traits, many being what Bem[49] termed androgynous. It was also possible that the differences being found between men and women in organizations were not due to gender at all but reflected their relative power status. That is, women being almost exclusively in positions that were subordinate to men, behaved in ways that were more conciliatory and more appropriate for a person with the lesser power.[50]

Research conducted within a liberal feminist perspective also reported on women occupying task-oriented roles or men utilizing person-oriented approaches.[51] This provides further evidence supporting the view that the so-called feminine and masculine leadership styles were not necessarily linked to individuals of those genders (although this is often assumed to be the case). Eagly and her colleagues[52] conducted meta-analyses with a view to determining whether or not there were gender differences in leadership styles. The 1990 meta-analysis found that leadership styles were slightly gender stereotypic for interpersonal style and democratic/autocratic, although effect sizes were not large. They found, additionally, that sex differences in style were less stereotypic in organizational settings than in lab studies, which they attributed to the greater salience of the managerial role in the organizational setting. Interestingly, they also found that, when considering the entire research literature, "women's leadership styles emphasize both interpersonal relations *and task accomplishment* to a slightly greater extent than men's styles"[53] (emphasis added). Task accomplishment is still viewed as a masculine leadership orientation.

Eagly and Johannesen-Schmidt's 2001 study[54] updated the earlier research by including more recent leadership formulations: transactional, transformational, and laissez-faire leadership styles. They again found small but significant differences in styles with women exceeding men on transformational scales and on the transactional scale of contingent rewards. Men exceeded women on transactional scales that are currently viewed as less positive (e.g., laissez-faire and passive management by exception), although they noted that while men were rated higher on these scales, ratings were generally low for both men and women.

These results, which suggested that women not only exhibit somewhat different styles but that these styles are indeed superior to those of men, is typical of what has been termed a *radical feminist* perspective[55] on gender and leadership. In this perspective, women's ways of leading include consensus building, participation, sharing information, concern about a supportive work environment, and commitment to diversity. Women's ways focus on collaboration, compared to men's ways that focus on power and problem solving.[56] In contrast to a liberal perspective, this approach moved away from notions of equality by suggesting that not only are women's ways different, they are superior to men's ways and should be valued and rewarded by organizations.

Doing Gender and Leadership

A social constructionist perspective[57] generally refers to how people actively construct their perceptions and develop mutual understandings of their world or what they consider to be reality. Lorber argued that while gender is supposedly based on the biological dichotomy between two sexes, our construction of what constitutes male and female is socially produced.[58] A social construction perspective on gender and leadership argues that dominance and subordination of men and women respectively are produced by our social constructions of gender and relationships. These constructions are so inculcated in people throughout their lives that they constitute part of their identity. Everyone 'does gender' almost all the time and, according to West & Zimmerman,[59] doing gender is unavoidable because of the pervasive social consequences of sex category membership in all spheres of life.

Gherardi discussed doing gender as handling the dual presence of men and women 'in such a way that we do not subvert the fundamental gender beliefs of our society"[60] and described the "celebration of the symbolic order of gender as the archetype of separateness ... between what is male and what is female and the 'symbolic' subordination of the latter to the former".[61] She suggested "women's lack of an assertive style can be interpreted as a ritual which repairs the offence caused by the infringement of the symbolic order of gender when they speak".[62] In other words, women are not supposed to infringe on the male territory of, for example, speaking up assertively in meetings. Women 'do gender' by either not speaking up or by being apologetic or tentative when doing so because of their socially constructed and inherently subordinate standing. This symbolic, subordinate position is clearly at odds with the notion of women as leaders.

Social construction explanations for issues associated with women and leadership are generally intuitively appealing and appear to be supported by much of the literature, although not necessarily explicitly. The history of leadership research itself supports a social constructionist perspective. The early leadership research, whether trait, behavioural, or situational, rarely if ever referred to either women or feminine attributes. Social constructions of the day did not allow for women or feminine ideas to impinge on leadership matters. Accordingly, a dichotomy of traits or behaviours was perceived and described on functional lines as person-oriented and task-oriented. No gender attributions were made about these behaviours and those who were considered the best leaders under these theories were those who combined task (initiating structure) and person (consideration) behaviours.

As women entered managerial and other leadership-oriented fields in the workplace, research responded with studies on how, and later why, women were different from men. The constructions of that time, circa 1970-1980, were that women exhibited a number of characteristics, such as caring, emotionality, and dependence that indicated a lack of suitability for leadership roles. As it became obvious that women were indeed in such roles, specific traits, characteristics, and behaviours came to be labelled as masculine or feminine, and were superimposed upon the existing dichotomy of task and person orientations. The very use of terminology such as feminine and masculine leadership styles for what were previously identified as task-oriented and person-oriented leadership behaviours, which are not sex determined, further supports the view of a continuing social construction of workplace behaviours and leadership along gendered lines.

Through the 1980s and 1990s, issues of human rights, equality, and feminism were increasingly prevalent. The Canadian Human Rights Act[63] came into law in 1977 and the Employment Equity Act[64] in 1995. This increase in rights issues corresponded to research themes that either claimed there were no gender differences with respect to leadership or that there were such differences but women's ways were better. This interaction of societal attitudes towards women and leadership and the research findings further supports the social constructionist perspective, particularly with respect to research on changing (albeit slowly) stereotypes of men and women leaders.

The popular and academic literatures are but two of the many sociocultural contributions to social constructions of women and leadership. Eagly and Johnson suggested that the leadership trait and style differences attributed to men and women were largely to be found in the popular literature for "practicing managers and the general public", while social scientists "generally maintained that there are in fact no reliable differences in the ways that women and men lead".[65] It is suggested here that the popular literature, which appears to be swayed in the direction of 'women's ways' is more widely read and may have more of a widespread impact on beliefs about women and leadership. The academic literature, which may be more rigorous and a closer approximation of 'the truth' is comparatively less widely read and potentially less likely to influence social construction of gender and leadership.

Those who have adopted the radical perspective[66] emphasized what are viewed as the interpersonal strengths of women. The "warmth, understanding, encouragement, support, nurturance, listening, empathy, and mutual trust"[67] Smith cites is distinctly at odds with the so-called masculine approach which is presumed to be strongly goal directed. The radical perspective exhorts women to capitalize on what they suggest are women's strengths and the advantages of women's ways. Indeed, the message is frequently so strong that it suggests that all leadership and organizational issues would be handily resolved through consensus building if only all leaders would adopt women's ways. It suggests, as Smith's chapter did, that *all* women have the talent for transformational leadership, seen by some to be a typically woman's style. Smith went so far as to suggest that women can understand the needs of their workers better and can therefore inspire loyalty in their employees better than men can, simply because of the way that "they, as women, have been socialized".[68]

This radical perspective suggests, again, that men and women are innately different with innately different behaviours. This is not supported by the literature, as noted earlier. While there are some small differences in the stereotypes of men's and women's leadership styles, the literature does not suggest that either feminine or masculine styles are innately female or male. Rather, the social constructionist view, which recognizes the continual production and reproduction of gender and gender appropriate behaviours, more adequately explains possible differences, as well as their evident changes over time.

Neither does the literature support a belief that men or women are inherently more effective leaders. Dipboye[69] found no consistent relationship between leader effectiveness and gender. Eagly, Karau, & Makhijani[70] similarly found that men and women leaders were equally effective. They noted, however, that leadership role congruence enhanced effectiveness. That is, women were more effective in leadership roles that required more of the so-called feminine leadership skills while men were more effective in typically male leadership roles. Similarly, men were more effective to the extent that leader and subordinate roles were male-dominated. This finding also supports a social constructionist perspective, with the construction occurring at the more proximal, workgroup level.

Conclusions

This chapter has linked the major themes of leadership research historically with the more recent research on gender and leadership. It has outlined the position of a number of theoretical perspectives on the issue of women and leadership and described how the history of both general leadership and women and leadership research supports a social constructionist view of gender and leadership.

Should women be leading like a man or adopting women's ways of leading? The radical feminist perspective described above would argue that women should capitalize on women's ways of leading. This not only highlights negligible differences and perpetuates stereotypes, many of them negative, about gender and leadership, but also claims vociferously that women's ways are better ways. Such an unsubstantiated bias does both men and women a disservice. It would also, likely, generate backlash from men, many of whom are in influential positions in organizations, who would receive the collateral message that 'men's ways are bad ways'. Attempting to capitalize solely on women's ways could also, further, serve to perpetuate the segregation of women into *pink ghettos* and such traditionally women dominated fields as human resources, rather than the more powerful leadership positions. The more that women behave in ways believed typical of their gender in leadership positions, the more that those constructions will be reinforced and perpetuated.

Rather it is suggested that women should neither lead like a man nor adopt women's ways of leading but should capitalize on the wealth of research and information on effective ways of leading men and women. While perhaps reminiscent of situational approaches to leadership, with the diverse workforces of today and the numerous forms of organizations and workgroups, it seems to make the most sense to lead in whatever manner is most effective for the team and the tasks at hand. This view is supported, in part, by Eagly and her colleagues'[71] finding that leadership effectiveness depends in part on features of the situation as well as attributes or styles of the leader.

Research to clarify the validity and utility of the different perspectives should be undertaken. While somewhat philosophical in nature, the questions of whether or not there are fundamental gender differences in leadership styles, attributes, ability, and effectiveness are basic questions that need to be resolved to both further our theoretical understanding and to provide concrete application for practitioners.

It is surprising that with so much research for so many years on leadership in general and regarding issues associated with women and leadership that more definitive answers have yet to be devised. The research on effectiveness with respect to gender issues in leadership, in particular, appears somewhat sparse and should be extended to include a variety of organizations, industries, and situational contexts as well as extending to more diverse group compositions.

ENDNOTES

1   Marilyn Loden, *Feminine Leadership; or, How to Succeed in Business Without Being One of the Boys*. (New York, NY: Times Books, 1985).

2   Susan Faludi, "Backlashes Then and Now". *Backlash: The Undeclared War on American Women.* (New York, NY: Crown, 1991).

3   Sally Helgesen, "Women's Ways of Leading". *The Female Advantage.* (New York: Bantam, 1990).

4   Kathleen Hall Jamieson, *Beyond the Double Bind: Women and Leadership.* (New York: Oxford University Press, 1995).

5   Bernard M. Bass, *Bass & Stogdill's Handbook of Leadership: Theory, Research, and Managerial Applications* (3rd ed.). (New York: The Free Press, 1990).

6   Rosabeth Moss Kanter, *Men and Women of the Corporation*. (New York, NY: Basic Books, 1977).

7   Karen Korabik, *Strangers in a Strange Land: Women Managers and the Legitimization of Authority*. Paper presented at the CPA annual meeting in Montreal, (May 29, 1993).

8   Judith Lorber, *Gender Inequality: Feminist Theories and Politics* (2nd ed.). (Los Angeles, CA: Roxbury Publishing Company, 2001).

9   Nathalie Rinfret, *Are Women Managers Agents of Change?* Paper presented at the CPA annual meeting in Quebec, QC, 2001.

10   Bass, *Handbook of Leadership*.

11   See Bass, *Handbook of Leadership*; Ralph M. Stogdill, *A Survey of Theory and Research*. (New York: The Free Press, 1974).

12   Ralph M. Stogdill, "Leadership, Membership and Organization". *Psychological Bulletin*, 47 (1950), 10.

13   Bass, *Handbook of Leadership*.

14   For example, Robert Hogan, Gordon J. Curphy, and Joyce Hogan, "What We Know About Leadership". *American Psychologist*, 49 (6, 1994), 493-504.

15   Paul Hersey, and Kenneth H. Blanchard, *Management of Organizational Behaviour* (5th ed.). (New Jersey: Prentice-Hall, 1988), 86.

16   Fred E. Fiedler, "The Contingency Model and the Dynamics of the Leadership Process". In L. Berkowitz (Ed.), *Advances in Experimental Social Psychology*, Volume 11. (New York: Academic Press, 1978).

17   David C. McClelland, "Toward a Theory of Motive Acquisition". *American Psychologist*, 20 (1960), 321-333.

18   Jeanette N. Cleveland, Margaret S. Stockdale, & Kevin R. Murphy, *Women and Men in Organizations: Sex and Gender Issues at Work*. (Mahwah, NJ: Lawrence Erlbaum Associates, 2000).

19   See Hogan, et al, What We Know About Leadership"; R. G. Lord, C. L. De Vader, and G. M. Alliger, G. M., "A Meta-analysis of the Relation Between Personality Traits and Leadership: An Application of Validity Generalization Procedures". *Journal of Applied Psychology*, 71 (1986), 402-410; Ralph M. Stogdill, "Personality Factors Associated with Leadership: A Survey of the Literature" *Journal*

of Psychology, 25 (1948), 35-71; Gary. A. Yukl, *Leadership in Organizations.* (Englewood Cliffs, New Jersey: Prentice-Hall, 1981).

20   M. R. Barrick, and M. K. Mount, "The Big Five Personality Dimensions and Job Performance: A Meta-analysis". *Personnel Psychology*, 44 (1991), 1-27.

21   R. R. McCrae, and P. Costa, "The Structure of Interpersonal Traits: Wiggins Circumplex and the Five-Factor Model". *Journal of Personality and Social Psychology*, 56, (1989), 586-595.

22   R. P. Tett, D. N. Jackson, and M. Rothstein, "Personality Measures as Predictors of Job Performance: A Meta-analytic Review". *Personnel Psychology*, 44, (1991), 703-742.

23   Ralph M. Stogdill, and A. E. Coons, *Leader Behaviour: Its Description and Measurement.* (Columbus, OH: Ohio State University, Bureau of Business Research, 1957).

24   R. R. Blake and J. S. Mouton, *The Managerial Grid.* (Houston, TX: Gulf, 1964).

25   Hersey and Blanchard, *Organizational Behaviour:* Stogdill, *Survey of Theory and Research.*

26   Hersey & Blanchard, *Organizational Behaviour.*

27   Stogdill, *Survey of Theory and Research*, 82.

28   Stogdill, *Survey of Theory and Research.*

29   Yukl, *Leadership in Organizations.*

30   G. W. Fairholm, *Values Leadership: Toward a New Philosophy of Leadership.* (New York: Praeger, 1991).

31   Tom Jaap, *Enabling Leadership: Achieving Results with People* (2nd ed.). (Vermont: Gower, 1989).

32   Bernard M. Bass, *Leadership and Performance Beyond Expectations.* (New York: The Free Press, 1985).

33   B. S. Pawar and K. K. Eastman, "The Nature and Implications of Contextual Influences on Transformational Leadership: A Conceptual Examination." *Academy of Management Review*, 22 (1, 1997), 80-109.

34   Bass, *Leadership and Performance Beyond Expectations.*

35   Douglas McGregor, *The Professional Manager.* (New York: McGraw-Hill, 1957), 23, as cited in V. E. O'Leary, "Some Attitudinal Barriers to Occupational Aspirations in Women." *Psychological Bulletin*, 81 (11, 1974), 811.

36   Jerry A. Jacobs, *Revolving Doors: Sex Segregation and Women's Careers.* (Stanford, CA: Stanford University Press, 1989); Barbara F. Reskin, and Irene Padavic, *Women and Men at Work.* (Thousand Oaks, CA: Pine Forge Press, 1994).

37   V. E. Schein, "The Relationship Between Sex Role Stereotypes and Requisite Management Characteristics". *Journal of Applied Psychology*, 57 (2, 1973), 95-100; V. E. Schein, "Relationships Between Sex Role Stereotypes and Requisite Management Characteristics Among Female Managers". *Journal of Applied Psychology*, 60 (3, 1975), 340-344.

38   J. Brenner, J. Tomiewics, and V. E. Schein, "The Relationship Between Sex Role Stereotypes and Requisite Management Characteristics. *Academy of Management Journal*, 32 (3, 1989), 662-669.

39   McGregor, *The Professional Manager.*

40   S. Halford and P. Leonard, *Gender, Power and Organisations: An Introduction.* (New York: Palgrave, 2001), 20.

41   O'Leary, *Attitudinal Barriers.*

42   Blake & Mouton, *Managerial Grid.*

43   Stogdill and Coons, *Leader Behaviour.*

44   The debate on leadership versus management is beyond the scope of this paper. I have avoided much of the 'women and management' literature because many of those publications are popular, non-academic writings. However, where deemed suitable (e.g., the introduction) publications on management or managers have been cited as have feminist writings from the popular and academic spheres.

45   See M. Gardiner and M. Tiggemann, "Gender Differences in Leadership Style, Job Stress and Mental Health in Male- and Female-dominated Industries". *Journal of Occupational and Organizational Psychology*, 72, (1999), 301-315; D. M. Smith, "Gender and Leadership Style". *Women at Work: Leadership for the Next Century.* (Upper Saddle River, NJ: Prentice-Hall, 2000).

46   Helgesen, "Women's Ways of Leading".

47   Smith, "Gender and Leadership Style".

153

48 Halford and Leonard, *Gender, Power, and Organizations*.

49 Sandra L. Bem, "Sex role adaptability: One consequence of psychological androgyny". *Journal of Personality and Social Psychology*, 31 (1975), 634-643.

50 Kanter, *Men and Women of the Corporation*.

51 For example, Korabik, *Strange Land*.

52 Alice H. Eagly & B. T. Johnson, "Gender and Leadership Styles: A Meta-analysis". *Psychological Bulletin*, 108 (2), 251-273, as reprinted in R. M. Steers, L. W. Porter, & G. A. Bigley, *Motivation and Leadership at Work*. (New York: McGraw-Hill, 1990); Alice H. Eagly, and M. C. Johannesen-Schmidt, "The leadership styles of women and men". *Journal of Social Issues*, 57 (4, 2001), 781-797.

53 Eagly and Johnson, "Gender and Leadership Styles, p. 265.

54 Eagly and Johannesen-Schmidt, "The leadership styles of women and men".

55 Lorber, *Feminist Theories and Politics*.

56 See Judy B. Rosener, Ways Women Lead. *Harvard Business Review*, (Nov/Dec 1990), 119-125; Smith, "Gender and Leadership Style".

57 Peter L. Berger, and Thomas Luckman, *The Social Construction of Reality*. (New York: Irvington, 1980); Kenneth J. Gergen, "The Social Constructionist Movement in Modern Psychology." *American Psychologist*, 40, (1985), 255-265.

58 Judith Lorber, "Dismantling Noah's Ark". *Sex Roles*, 14, (1986), 567-580; Lorber, *Feminist Theories and Politics*.

59 C. West and D. H. Zimmerman, "Doing Gender". *Gender & Society*, 1 (1987), 125-151.

60 Sylvia Gherardi, *Gender, symbolism, and organizational cultures*. (London, England: SAGE, 1995), 129.

61 Ibid, 137.

62 Ibid, 141.

63 Canada. Canadian Human Rights Act, S. C. 1976-77, c.33, as amended, 1977.

64 Canada. Employment Equity (EE) Act, 1995.

65 Eagly and Johnson, "Gender and Leadership Styles".

66 For example, Smith, "Gender and Leadership Style".

67 Smith, "Gender and Leadership Style", 41.

68 Ibid.

69 Robert L. Dipboye, "Problems and Progress of Women in Management". In K. S. Koziara, M. H. Moskow, and L. D. Tanner (Eds.), *Working Women: Past, Present, Future.* (Washington, DC: Bureau of National Affairs, 1987).

70 Alice H. Eagly, S. J. Karau, and M. G. Makhijani, "Gender and the Effectiveness of Leaders: A Meta-Analysis". *Psychological Bulletin*, 117 (1995), 125-145.

71 Ibid.

CHAPTER 10

Special Program for Female Selection to Canadian Forces Command and Staff Course

Dr. Irina Goldenberg and Lieutenant-Commander Gordon AuCoin

Canadian Forces Command and Staff Course (CFCSC) is a one-year course offered through the Canadian Defence Academy to prepare new Lieutenant-Colonels/Commanders and senior Majors/Lieutenant-Commanders for senior staff appointments and command positions in the Canadian Forces (CF). Each year, approximately 100 individuals are selected to attend (with approximately 15 of these positions designated for foreign staff colleges). Set numbers of seats are allocated for specific military occupations (MOCs), with approximately 60 seats designated for CF members in operational MOCs, 40 for members in non-operational MOCs, with two to three seats reserved for members in specialist MOCs.[1]

The CFCSC selection board is responsible for selecting the candidates who will attend the course. When individuals are selected for the course, they may attend, have their attendance deferred until the following year because of operational reasons, or refuse to attend. The selection procedure for CFCSC entails career managers preparing nomination lists by MOC and presenting these lists to the CFCSC selection board, as well as briefing the board on reasons for not recommending a member, deferral requests, or requirements for additional seats. At the top of the lists are members deferred from the previous year. Using this information, lists of the top eligible[2] members are created for each MOC, in order of merit from the latest promotion selection board. These lists of candidates are long enough to ensure that all available seats are filled once deferrals and refusals to attend are taken into account (approximately two to three times the number of seats available).[3] Thus, to complete the lists of potential candidates, career managers add additional officers "based on performance, potential, and Environmental Chiefs of Staff (ECS) Branch input".[4] The final lists comprise both primary and alternate candidates.[5]

Historically, women were less likely to meet the prerequisites for attendance to CFCSC because women who enrolled prior to 1989 were excluded from serving in operational occupations, while approximately 60 percent of the CFCSC positions are designated for those serving in these operational occupations.[6] In 1997, a special selection program for selecting additional women to attend CFCSC was implemented as a measure to eliminate this barrier to equitable career development opportunities for female officers.

Thus, in addition to the primary and alternate candidate lists described above, a female list is created in order to fill up to five additional seats with the five most deserving female candidates that would not otherwise be selected.[7] The selection board derives this additional female list by ranking the top female candidates who meet the basic Staff College student profile and who are not on the primary lists (those on the alternate lists may also be on the special measure list).[8]

The numbers of women that have attended CFCSC from both the regular and the special measures female lists between 2000 and 2005 are presented in Table 1. As shown, the absolute number of women that attended from the female list has decreased steadily since 2000, and the proportion of women that attended from the regular list has increased, in general.

Table 1: Total Female Attendants by Selection List

Selection List	2000	2001	2002	2003	2004	2005
Regular List	2	3	3	2	2	5
Female List	5	4	3	3	3	2
Total	7	7	6	5	5	7
% Females from Regular List	28.6	42.9	50.0	40.0	40.0	71.4

Initially, the special measures program was to be in effect for approximately three years. Since 2002, the Directorate of Human Rights and Diversity

(DHRD)[9] has reviewed this program on an annual basis to monitor the number of women attending and to determine whether or not the special measures program is still required. The recommendations from these reviews indicated that the program should be continued and that DHRD should continue to review the requirement for the program on an annual basis. In addition, a more in-depth analysis (i.e., beyond the annual comparison of the number of men and women eligible and number of men and women who attended CFCSC) was requested.[10]

This investigation was conducted in order to:

1. Assess if men and women have different utilization rates of CFCSC by comparing their rates of eligibility and rates of attendance;

2. Explore if differences in utilization rates may stem from differences on key variables of interest between the men and women who were eligible, as well as between men and women who were selected;[11] and

3. Compare the rates at which men and women who were selected,
   a. attended CFCSC;
   b. had their attendance deferred for operational reasons; or
   c. refused to attend.

Eligibility and Attendance at CFCSC: A Comparison of Male and Female Utilization Rates

Men's and women's eligibility rates and attendance rates to CFCSC were examined in order to assess their comparability. Further, an analysis of adverse impact was conducted as an indicator of possible barriers impeding female attendance at CFCSC. Adverse impact is a statistically measurable result of an employment practice or process that disproportionately excludes target group members,[12] in this case women. A practical standard that serves as a test of adverse impact is the 80 percent rule; thus, if female utilization rates for CFCSC do not fall within 20 percent or 4/5ths of male rates, there is an indication of adverse impact.

Eligibility data for CFCSC was obtained from the Human Resource Management System (HRMS) and attendance data for CFCSC was obtained from the CFCSC selection board secretary. This data spanned the years between 2000 and 2005. Female share of eligibility for selection to CFCSC was calculated by dividing the number of eligible women by the total number of eligible CF members. Similarly, female share of attendance to CFCSC was calculated by dividing the number of women that attended by the total number of CF members that attended. Utilization rates to CFCSC were calculated by dividing the number of men or women that attended the program by the number of men or women who were eligible. Adverse impact ratios were calculated by dividing female utilization rates by male utilization rates.

The calculations yielded the following results:

Female Share of Eligibility: The female share of those eligible to attend CFCSC hovered between 5 and 6 percent between 2000 and 2003, but increased to 8 percent in 2004 and 2005 (Table 2);

Female Share of Attendance: However, a somewhat reverse pattern occurred with respect to the female share of those attended the program (Table 2). In particular, female shares of attendees were highest in 2000 and 2001, at 8 percent, and began to decline to 7 percent in 2002, and dropped to just 5 percent in 2003 and 2004. These attendance rates rebounded somewhat to 7 percent in 2005, with seven female attendees for the first time since 2001.

Utilization Rates: Given these reverse patterns between the shares of female eligibility and female attendance, it is not surprising that although the female utilization rate was higher than the male utilization rate between 2000 and 2002, the reverse pattern is observed between 2003 and 2005, where the male utilization rates exceeded the female utilization rates (Table 2).

Consequently, the adverse impact ratio has been below 1.0 as of 2003, although 2004 was the only year in which this ratio was below the 0.8 indicator for significant adverse impact (i.e., women's utilization rate was not within 20 percent of men's utilization rate). Given that seven women attended in 2005, the adverse impact ratio for this most recent year did not fall below the 0.8 guideline, but was still below 1.0, indicating that the female utilization rate remained below the male utilization rate. Overall, this data indicates that women's attendance at CFCSC has not been moving in a positive direction in recent years. Although more women are becoming eligible, the number of women actually attending the program has not been increasing at the same rate.

Table 2: Eligibility and Attendance Rates to CFCSC by Sex

		Female	Male	Total	Female Share	Adverse Impact Ratio
2005	Eligible	67	784	851	0.08	
	Attended[a]	7	93	100	0.07	0.9
	Utilization Rate	10.4%	11.9%	11.8%		
2004	Eligible	53	629	682	0.08	
	Attended	5	91	96	0.05	0.6
	Utilization Rate	9.4%	14.5%	14.1%		
2003	Eligible	33	507	540	0.06	
	Attended	5	89	94	0.05	0.9
	Utilization Rate	15.2%	17.6%	17.4%		
2002	Eligible	26	480	506	0.05	
	Attended	6	84	90	0.07	1.3
	Utilization Rate	23.1%	17.5%	17.8%		
2001	Eligible	31	474	505	0.06	
	Attended	7	84	91	0.08	1.3
	Utilization Rate	22.6%	17.7%	18.0%		
2000	Eligible	30	472	502	0.06	
	Attended	7	84	91	0.08	1.3
	Utilization Rate	23.3%	17.8%	18.1%		

[a]Includes women from both the regular and special selection/female list

Occupational Stream Analysis of Eligibility and Attendance to CFCSC

The occupational streams (i.e., operational, non-operational, specialist) from which women and men were eligible, and from which men and women attended, were examined. Adverse impact analyses were not conducted at this level, with the exception of the non-operational occupational stream, because the small numbers of women precludes the capacity to make meaningful observations.

The great majority of women eligible for CFCSC between 2000 and 2005 were in non-operational military occupations, followed by specialist occupations, with the fewest number of women being employed in the operational occupations (Table 3). The pattern is quite different with respect to men's eligibility. Although the majority of eligible men were also in the non-operational occupations, this is followed quite closely by the number of eligible men in the operational occupations, with proportionally far fewer eligible men coming from the specialist occupations.

The majority of women who attended CFCSC between 2000 and 2005 were in non-operational occupations (Table 3). In fact, 2005 was the first year that a woman attended from either an operational or a specialist occupation (although there are only two to three positions reserved for individuals from the specialist occupational stream each year). By contrast, the majority of men who attended came from the operational occupations, despite the fact that as for women (albeit to a far lesser extent), there were more men than women eligible in the non-operational occupations.

Thus, the occupations from which men and women were eligible for selection, and from which men and women attended, differ substantially. Most eligible women were in the non-operational occupations, and indeed, most women who attended were from this occupational stream. In contrast, although most eligible men were also in the non-operational occupations (although to a far lesser extent than is the case for women), the majority of men who attended come from the operational occupational stream.

Table 3: Eligibility and Attendance Rates by Occupational Stream and by Sex

		Operational			Non-Operational			Specialist		
		Female	Male	Female Share	Female	Male	Female Share	Female	Male	Female Share
2005	Eligible	4	321	0.01	49	411	0.11	14	52	0.21
	Attended[a]	1	56	0.02	5	36	0.12	1	1	0.50
2004	Eligible	3	238	0.01	41	347	0.11	9	44	0.17
	Attended	0	53	0.00	5	37	0.12	0	1	0.00
2003	Eligible	1	204	0.00	27	295	0.08	5	8	0.38
	Attended	0	48	0.00	5	40	0.11	0	1	0.00
2002	Eligible	0	189	0.00	23	283	0.08	3	8	0.27
	Attended	0	49	0.00	6	33	0.15	0	2	0.00
2001	Eligible	0	172	0.00	28	294	0.09	3	8	0.27
	Attended	0	51	0.00	7	31	0.18	0	2	0.00
2000	Eligible	0	170	0.00	28	295	0.09	2	7	0.22
	Attended	0	50	0.00	7	32	0.18	0	2	0.00

[a]Total females selected includes women from both the regular and special selection/female list.

Eligibility and Attendance in the Non-Occupational Stream

Since most of the women that were eligible and that attended CFCSC were in the non-operational occupations, and there are sufficient numbers of women for analysis, a specific examination of men's and women's eligibility and attendance rates in this occupational stream was conducted. The analysis of results yielded the following:

Female Share of Eligibility: The female share of those eligible in the non-operational stream dropped from 9 percent in 2000 and 2001, to 8 percent in 2002 and 2003, but increased again to 11 percent in 2004 and 2005 (Table 4).

Female Share of Attendance: The pattern with respect to the female share of those that attended was quite different, with the female share of attendees decreasing from 18 percent in 2000 and 2001 to 12 percent by 2004 and 2005. Thus, although generally more women in non-operational occupations are becoming eligible for CFCSC over time, their attendance rates are actually decreasing.

This is the same pattern that is observed in overall changes over time in women's eligibility and attendance, across all three occupational streams combined.

Utilization Rates: These increases in eligibility rates and decreases in attendance rates for women in the non-operational occupations are evidenced in the resultant utilization rates, and the adverse impact ratios comparing the utilization rates of men and women, both of which have generally decreased over the years. Nevertheless, there is certainly no indication of adverse impact, and women's utilization rates, although lower than they were in earlier years, continue to exceed men's utilization rates in the non-operational occupational stream.

Table 4: Eligibility and Attendance Rates by Sex in Non-Operational Occupations

		Female	Male	Total	Female Share	Adverse Impact Ratio
2005	Eligible	49	411	460	0.11	
	Attended[a]	5	36	41	0.12	1.2
	Utilization Rate	10.2%	8.8%	8.9%		
2004	Eligible	41	347	388	0.11	
	Attended	5	37	42	0.12	1.1
	Utilization Rate	12.2%	10.7%	10.8%		
2003	Eligible	27	295	322	0.08	
	Attended	5	40	45	0.11	1.4
	Utilization Rate	18.5%	13.6%	14.0%		
2002	Eligible	23	283	306	0.08	
	Attended	6	33	39	0.15	2.2
	Utilization Rate	26.1%	11.7%	12.7%		
2001	Eligible	28	294	322	0.09	
	Attended	7	31	38	0.18	2.4
	Utilization Rate	25.0%	10.5%	11.8%		
2000	Eligible	28	295	323	0.09	
	Attended	7	32	39	0.18	2.3
	Utilization Rate	25.0%	10.8%	12.1%		

[a]Total females selected includes women from both the regular and special selection/female list.

Characteristics of Those Eligible and Selected for CFCSC: Comparison by Sex

Exploratory analyses were conducted to assess possible differences between men (n = 2535; 92.2 percent) and women (n = 214; 7.8 percent) who were eligible for selection to CFCSC, as well as between men (n = 558; 95.1 percent) and women (n = 29; 4.9 percent) who were selected to attend[13] between 2002 and 2005. Detected differences may point to reasons for why different attendance rates would be expected between men and women. Alternatively differences may be indicative of barriers to women's selection for CFCSC.

Men and women who were eligible for selection to CFCSC, as well as men and women who were selected to attend CFCSC, were compared on the following variables[14]: years of service; age; days of leave without pay; first official language; marital status; and whether or not they had dependent children. Individuals eligible for CFCSC were identified through HRMS and individuals who were selected to attend were identified through consultation with the CFCSC selection board secretary.[15] Data on the variables of interest for individuals from both groups were obtained through HRMS as follows:

Years of Service: On average, men eligible for CFCSC had more years of service than women who were eligible (x = 20.4, sd = 4.3 versus x = 18.0, sd = 4.8, for men and women, respectively). Similarly, men selected for CFCSC had more years of service than women who were selected (x = 19.8, sd = 3.6 versus x =19.0, sd =3.5, for men and women, respectively), although this difference was smaller than the difference between eligible men and women. These findings point to one, albeit minor, possible reason for why men may be selected to attend at higher rates than women, but does not indicate a barrier to women's attendance.

Age: On average, men eligible for CFCSC were slightly older than eligible women (x = 41.2, sd = 3.9 versus x = 40.5, sd = 4.1, for men and women, respectively). However, the reverse pattern was observed with respect to the average age of selected men and women (x = 40.5, sd = 3.5 and x = 41.1, sd = 3.4, for men and women, respectively). Given the small magnitudes in the age differences, combined with the finding that selected men have more years of service, this pattern of results does not indicate a barrier for women's attendance to CFCSC.

Days of Leave Without Pay: On average, eligible women had taken a much greater number of days of leave without pay than did eligible men (x = 112.3, sd = 98.1 versus x = 44.9, sd = 165.3, for women and men, respectively). Similarly, women who were selected to attend CFCSC had much higher periods of leave without pay than did men who were selected (x = 127.21, sd = 294.3 versus x = 37.7, sd = 66.4, for women and men, respectively). This difference probably stems from women's greater likelihood to take maternity/parental leave. Despite this large difference between men and women in the number of days without pay, this pattern of results, in itself, does not indicate that the number of days without pay has a negative effect on women's attendance to CFCSC. In fact, the women who were selected to attend had a greater number of days of leave without pay than the general pool of eligible women (although the variability in the former group with respect to number of days without pay was very high).

First Official Language: There was practically no difference in first official language between eligible men and eligible women, and English was the first official language for approximately three quarters of both groups (Table 5). However, there was a difference in first official language between the men and women who were selected for CFCSC, with English being the first official language for a greater proportion of the women. For men, the proportion of native English and French speakers was very similar between those who were eligible and those that were selected. By contrast, the proportion of native English speakers was far higher in the women selected than in the pool of women who were eligible. This points to a potential barrier to women's attendance, particularly to the attendance of French women. It is possible that the challenges associated with being a minority group with respect to both sex and official language diminish the number of French women who are selected to attend CFCSC, and ultimately reduce the overall number of women who attend. However, given that the magnitude of this difference is not particularly large, combined with the small number of women selected, this finding ought to be interpreted with caution.

Table 5: First Official Language by Sex

	Eligible for CFCSC		Selected for CFCSC	
	Men	Women	Men	Women
English	72.1%	72.4%	74.1%	89.7%
French	27.9%	27.6%	25.9%	10.3%

Marital Status: There were some clear differences in marital status between men and women who were eligible for CFCSC (Table 6). Eligible men were more likely to be married or common law than eligible women (although this was the most prevalent marital status for both groups),[16] whereas eligible women were more likely to be either single or divorced/separated than eligible men. The pattern of differences in marital status between the men and women who were selected for CFCSC was similar to that of men and women who were eligible for selection, but these differences were even more pronounced in some areas. In particular, selected women were even less likely to be married or common law than the selected men, and they were even more likely to be divorced or separated.

Perhaps most revealing were the differences between women who were eligible and women who were selected. The proportion of selected women who were married or common law was lower than in the larger pool of eligible women (whereas for men there was almost no difference between those eligible and those selected). By contrast, the proportion of selected women who were divorced or separated was higher than in the pool of women who were eligible (whereas for men, again there was almost no difference).

This pattern of results is indicative of a possible barrier to women's attendance to CFCSC. It appears that, in general, it is more difficult for women to 'have it all' with respect to balancing the demands of marriage and career than it is for men. This is the case for women in general – that is, for both women who were selected to CFCSC and those in the larger pool of eligible women, which in itself may be indicative of a barrier to women's selection to CFCSC and to women's career progression in the CF in general. However, this challenge appears to be particularly pronounced in the women who were actually selected to attend. It seems that for these women, who arguably excelled most in their careers, there was an even greater difficulty to balance the demands of marriage and career. By contrast, selected men did not seem to have this same challenge, as evidenced by the lack of difference between them and the men in the larger eligible pool.

Table 6: Marital Status by Sex

	Eligible for CFCSC		Selected for CFCSC	
	Men	Women	Men	Women
Married/Common Law	92.8%	69.6%	93.7%	62.0%
Divorced/Separated	3.5%	10.3%	3.3%	17.2%
Single	3.4%	20.1%	3.1%	17.2%
Widowed	0.2%	0.0%	0.0%	3.4%

Dependent Children: The results of whether or not members had dependent children were consistent with the results for marital status. In particular, women (both eligible and selected) were less likely to have dependent children than were men (Table 7). Futhermore, whereas the selected women were slightly less likely to have dependent children than women from the larger eligibility pool, there was almost no difference between eligible and selected men. This further indicates that it may be more difficult for women to balance the demands of family and career, and that this challenge may be even more pronounced for women who excel in their career.

Table 7: Dependent Children by Sex

	Eligible for CFCSC		Selected for CFCSC	
	Men	Women	Men	Women
Percentage w/Children	87.0%	64.5%	85.7%	58.6%

Attendance and Rate of Refusal: A Comparison by Sex

When individuals are selected for the course, they may attend, have their attendance deferred until the following year because of operational reasons, or refuse to attend. Refusal to attend is seriously frowned upon and has negative impacts on the officer's career.[17] However, it is thought that women refuse to attend at greater rates than men.[18]

According to the recent CF Employment Systems Review (ESR), "there is a great deal of stigma attached to the additional list by both male and some female peers, the inference being that the offer to attend CFCSC and subsequent potential for promotion is not based on meritorious performance,"[19] and the extra female list is often referred to as the *pink list* in common parlance. Further, it was reported that some female nominees have refused offers to attend the program because they do not want to be perceived or labeled as having been chosen on a special basis. However, this information is based on anecdotal evidence, and the true extent to which women are deterred from attending because of the special measure requires further investigation. Indeed, the ESR found that both female and male officers refuse offers to attend the program for personal reasons, such as having reached an age and point in their careers where they wish to devote more time to family and not have the additional challenges associated with promotion to a higher rank.

Analyses were conducted to verify whether women do in fact refuse to attend CFCSC at greater rates than men. The available data specify whether the individual refused to attend the program, but do not specify the reason for the refusal. However, if these findings indicate that women refused to attend at greater rates than men, this would point to the need for further examination to assess whether they are indeed refusing as a result of the stigma associated with the female list.

Individuals who were selected to attend[20] were identified through consultation with the CFCSC selection board secretary. Information regarding whether selected members came from a primary list, alternate list, or the female list,[21] along with information regarding whether each selected member actually attended, deferred their attendance for operational reasons, or refused to attend was also provided. This data spanned the years between 2002 and 2005.

A total of 558 men and 29[22] women were selected to attend CFCSC between 2002 and 2005. The rates at which selected men and selected women either attended or did not attend the program were compared. Women who were selected for CFCSC attended the program at somewhat higher rates than did men who were selected to attend (Table 8).

Table 8: Attendance Rate of Selected Members by Sex

	Attended		Did Not Attend	
	Number	Percentage	Number	Percentage
Male	357	60.4%	201	36.0%
Female	22	75.9%	7	24.1%

The reasons for men's and women's non-attendance were compared among those who did not attend the program. The most prevalent reason for women's non-attendance was refusal, whereas the most prevalent reasons for men's non-attendance was operational reasons (although these analyses must be interpreted with particular caution due to the small number of women who refused to attend overall) (Table 9). Thus, although selected woman had higher rates of attendance than men, this may largely be attributed to the high proportion of men whose attendance was deferred for operational reasons, which is not surprising since a greater proportion of the men were selected from the operational occupations.

Table 9: Reason for Non-Attendance by Sex

	Refused		Operational Reason		Other[a]	
	Number	Percentage	Number	Percentage	Number	Percentage
Male	49	25.8%	125	65.8%	27	13.4%
Female	4	57.1%	1	14.3%	2	28.6%

[a]'Other' reasons include the member being released, being medically unfit, not having their OPME completed, and missing information.

Analyses were conducted to assess whether women's attendance rates differed depending on what list they were chosen from. Results indicated that women chosen from the primary lists had the highest rate of attendance, followed by women chosen from the female list, with women chosen from the alternate lists having the lowest attendance rates (although these analyses must be interpreted with particular caution due to the small number of women in each group) (Table 10).

Table 10: Female Attendance Rates by Selection List

Attendance	Primary List		Alternate List		Female List	
	Number	Percentage	Number	Percentage	Number	Percentage
Yes	8	100.0%	4	57.1%	10	71.4%
No	0	0.0%	3	42.9%	4	28.6%

Analyses were conducted on the subset of women who did not attend in order to compare the refusal rates of women chosen from the female and the alternate lists. Since all women selected from the primary list attended, they were not included in this analysis. Indeed, it was found that the women chosen from the female list refused to attend at higher rates than those chosen from the alternate lists (although these analyses must be interpreted with particular caution due to the small number of women in each group) (Table 11).

Table 11: Reason for Female Non-Attendance by Selection List

List	Refused		Operational		Other	
	Number	Percentage	Number	Percentage	Number	Percentage
Alternate	1	33.3%	1	33.3%	1	33.3%
Female	3	75.0%	0	0.0%	1	25.0%

Conclusion and Recommendations

Overall, the results of this analysis indicate that women's attendance at CFCSC has not been moving in a positive direction in recent years. Although more women are becoming eligible for attendance, the number of women actually attending the program has not been increasing at the same rate. Indeed, female utilization rates for attendance to CFCSC have been below male utilization rates for the past three years (i.e., since 2003). These findings indicate that the special measures program ought to be continued.

When the eligibility and attendance rates of only the non-operational occupations are examined, female utilization rates are higher than those of men. However, although more women in the non-operational occupations are becoming eligible for CFCSC over time, the attendance rates for women have actually decreased in recent years (similar to the overall pattern in women's eligibility and attendance, across all three occupational streams combined). This further indicates that the special measures program be continued, so that women's utilization rates do not fall below male utilization rates in the non-operational occupational stream, as they currently do in the CF overall (when all occupational streams are combined), and to compensate for these overall lower utilization rates.

Although the special selection program was originally implemented in order to address systemic barriers impeding the career development of female officers stemming from the exclusion of women in operational occupations prior to 1989, the vast majority of women eligible for CFCSC still come from the non-operational occupations. Furthermore, the representation rates of women in the operational occupations may never be as high as those of men – not necessarily because of organizational barriers to women's enrolment in these occupations, but also due to factors associated with women's interest and propensity to engage in these particular occupations, stemming from socialization and other societal factors.[23] Since currently approximately 60 of the seats to CFCSC are reserved for those in the operational occupations, these findings point to another reason for the continuation of the special selection measure, which will contribute to the advancement of women to senior CF staff appointments and command positions at a rate that is more similar to that of their male counterparts.

The absolute number of women that attended from the female list has decreased steadily since 2000, with all five of the possible extra seats being filled in 2000, four being filled in 2001, three being filled in 2002-2004, and only two of the five possible extra seats provided by the special measure being filled in 2005. Since the male utilization rates to CFCSC exceeded the female utilization rates between 2003 and 2005, it is recommended that better use be made of the special measure program such that enough women be selected from the special measures list (up to the maximum of five women) so that women's rates better match those of their male counterparts.

It seems that it is more difficult for women to 'have it all' with respect to balancing the demands of family and career. Women eligible for CFCSC were less likely to be married and more likely to be single, divorced, or separated, than eligible men, and they were less likely to have children. Moreover, this challenge of balancing the demands of family and career seems to be particularly pronounced in the women who were actually selected to attend CFCSC, and who arguably excelled most in their careers. These women were even less likely to be married and to have children, and were even more likely to be divorced or separated than women from the larger eligibility pool, whereas these disparities did not exist between eligible and selected men. In addition to the recommendations regarding female selection to CFCSC presented here, the continued progress made by the Directorate of Quality of Life, whose mission is to "monitor, promote and continuously improve the quality of life of CF members and their families"[24] and the Directorate of Human Rights and Diversity, who has the primary responsibility for CF policies and programs concerned with gender integration and employment equity,[25] may facilitate women's ability to balance the demands of family and career.

The recent ESR[26] found that although some CF members feel that the special selection measure is an important and justified employment equity initiative, others believe that it is not fair, may lead to stigma and perceptions that women are selected based on less rigorous standards, and that the measure should be dropped. Further, the ESR concluded that the main issue is not with the special selection measure itself, but rather with the general lack of understanding as to why positive measures such as this one exist for the purposes of employment equity. As a result of these findings, the ESR recommended that a Defence Administrative Order and Directive (DAOD) be developed to explain the CFCSC selection process and the special selection measure. Alternatively, an elaboration and re-promulgation of the CANFORGEN on the special selection measure may be a better way to serve this awareness-raising function.

The findings presented herein lend some further support for the above recommendation, although these findings ought to be interpreted with caution due to the small number of women. Although overall, women who were selected to attend actually attended at higher rates than selected men, of individuals that did not attend, men tended to have their attendance deferred for operational reasons, whereas women were more likely to refuse to attend. Although the rates of non-attendance were higher for women selected from the alternate list than for women selected from the female list, when the reason for non-attendance was considered, those on the female list did refuse to attend at greater rates than women on the alternate list. It may be that women selected from the female list did refuse to attend due to stigma attached with the special selection measure, or because they felt that their selection was not based solely on merit. For this reason, better communication is needed to explain the reason behind the existence of the special selection measure, particularly to the women who are selected in this manner and to all CFCSC participants. In addition, it would be worthwhile for career managers to query women with respect to whether their refusal did indeed stem from being chosen via the special measure, and this information should be relayed to the CFCSC selection board for use in future decision-making.

The purpose of the Employment Equity (EE) Act is "to achieve equality in the workplace so that no person shall be denied employment opportunities or benefits for reasons unrelated to ability and in the fulfillment of that goal, to correct the conditions of disadvantage in employment experienced by women, Aboriginal Peoples, persons with disabilities and members of visible minorities".[27] These four groups are referred to as designated group members (DGMs) in the EE Act. The ESR found that there are some barriers to the career advancement of Aboriginal People and visible minorities.[28] Thus, it is recommended that a similar review be conducted to assess whether there is equitable attendance to CFSCS for Aboriginal People and visible minorities. Because the need for all CF members to meet the requirements of universality of service affects the policies relating to the promotion and retention of persons with disabilities in the CF, a review for this group is not recommended at the present time.

ENDNOTES

1   Commander D. G. Cameron, Staff College Selection Board Career Manager Instructions. 5076-19-8 (DMCARM 7 Ed), (2004).

2   The Staff College student profile for eligibility to CFCSC includes being at minimum, at the rank of Maj/LCdr and having entered the promotion zone to being at the rank of Cdr/LCol as well as having completed the Officer Professional Military Education (OPME) program or equivalent (Skidmore, 2004).

3   Major L. Hatton, Personal communication (December 14, 2004); and Commander J.A. Roche, Staff College Selection. Briefing Note for ADM (HR-Mil), (2005).

4   Ibid.

5   Brigadier-General M.S. Skidmore, Staff College Selection Board Convening Order and Instructions. 5076-19-8 (DMCARM 7).

6   Commander D.G. Cameron, Staff College Selection Board Career Manager Instructions; and N. Holden, "An analysis of female selection for Canadian Forces Command and Staff Course" Briefing Note for DTEP, (2003).

7   Commander D.G. Cameron, Staff College Selection Board Career Manager Instructions; and Department of National Defence, *Selection Board 2005/2006 Board Report* (Toronto, ON: CFCSC Selection Board).

8   Commander D.G. Cameron, Staff College Selection Board Career Manager Instructions; and Major L. Hatton, Personal communication. (December 14, 2004).

9   Previously called the Directorate of Military Gender Integration and Employment Equity (DMGIEE).

10   Lieutenant-Colonel J.A. Paradis, Personal communication. (February 25, 2004).

11   Due to the small number of women who have been selected to attend CFCSC the results of this analysis should be interpreted with caution. Possible differences identified may point to a need for more in-depth or qualitative investigation

12   Department of National Defence, *The Canadian Forces Employment Equity Plan. Building Teamwork in a Diverse Canadian Forces,* (1999); and Human Resources and Social Development Canada, *CHRC Audit Procedures Manual,* Chapter 8. http://www.hrsdc.gc.ca/en/lp/lo/lswe/we/ee_tools/tools/chrc/026_chapter_8_2.shtml, (2005).

13 Tests of statistical significance were not conducted because analyses were based on the total populations of members eligible and selected for CFCSC, and were not based on sample statistics.

14 Comparisons based on level of education were also planned, but were not conducted due to the unreliability of the data (Capt K.A. Gonzalez, Personal Communication (November 3, 2005) HRMS (2005). HRMS Disclaimer for education data).

15 These lists were comprised of all the primary candidates on each list, as well as the alternate candidates on each that were actually selected to attend. Alternates candidates are selected to attend one at a time, in order of their position on the alternate lists, until the total number of seats allocated to their respective MOCs are filled when deferrals and refusals are taken into account.

16 This general pattern is also true for male and female Officers in the CF overall: 71.8 percent of all male Officers are married as compared to 52.6 percent of all female Officers (Employment Equity Management System. 2006).

17 Major L. Hatton, Personal communication (December 14, 2004).

18 Ajilon Consulting. *Canadian Forces Employment Systems Review*, 2004.

19 Ibid.

20 These lists were comprised of all the primary candidates on each list, as well as the alternate candidates on each that were actually invited to attend. Alternates candidates are invited to attend one at a time, in order of their position on the alternate lists, until the total number of seats allocated to their respective MOCs are filled when deferrals and refusals are taken into account.

21 Female candidates sometimes move between the alternate and female lists during the process of selection and filling of all the available CFCSC seats (Hatton, 2004). Information regarding which list members were selected from that was provided by the CFCSC selection board secretary was used for these analyses, and is the best available data in this regard.

22 Due to the small number of women who have been selected to attend CFCSC the results of this analysis should be interpreted with caution. Possible differences identified may point to a need for more in-depth or qualitative investigation.

23 L.B. Bradley, *A sociocultural and organizational level examination of occupational sex segregation* (Unpublished manuscript, 2002); and Irina Goldenberg, *A New Approach*

to Estimating Workforce Availability for the Canadian Forces (Ottawa, ON: Centre for Operational Research and Analysis and Director Human Rights and Diversity, 2005).

24   Directorate of Quality of Life (2005).

25   Directorate of Human Rights and Diversity. (2005). http://hr3.ottawa-hull.mil. ca/dmgiee/engraph/Home_e.asp.

26   Ajilon Consulting, *Canadian Forces Employment Systems Review.*

27   *The Employment Equity Act.* Section 2 (1995). http://laws.justice.gc.ca/en/E-5.401/49886.html.

28   Ajilon Consulting, Canadian Forces Employment Systems Review.

Contributors

Lieutenant-Commander **Gordon AuCoin** is a Maritime Surface (MARS) officer, currently employed within the Directorate of Human Rights and Diversity as the Canadian Forces Desk Officer for Gender Integration. His responsibilities include identification and elimination of systemic barriers that that may interfere with women having an equal opportunity to progress their careers in the Canadian Forces. Lieutenant-Commander AuCoin's military career spans more than 30 years and has included a variety appointments primarily focused in the areas of maritime operations and human resources.

Lieutenant-Commander **Lynn Bradley** (M. Sc., 1997, University of Calgary (Industrial Organizational Psychology)) began her career as an Army Radio Operator and then a Signals Officer in the Communication Reserve. She commanded 712 (Montreal) Communication Squadron before transferring to the Regular Force as a Personnel Selection Officer in 1991. Lieutenant-Commander Bradley is currently with the Maritime Staff as the Command Personnel Selection Officer, personnel policy analyst, and the Office of Primary Interest (OPI) for all personnel applied research and military psychology issues in the Navy. She has engaged in a variety of research activities over the past ten years, including the study on whether to employ women in Canadian submarines and an interview study on lessons learned in mixed gender ships, and has presented at national and international forums on the topics of gender integration and employment equity.

Lieutenant-Commander (retired) **Karen D. Davis** is a defence scientist with the Canadian Forces Leadership Institute and Centre for Operational Research and Analysis, and holds a Master of Arts in Sociology from McGill University. Karen joined the Canadian Forces in 1978 as an Oceanographic Operator, was commissioned in 1989 as a Personnel Selection Officer, and 'retired' in 2000. She has conducted research in the Canadian Forces and Department of National Defence for over 15 years on a range of human resource related issues including gender integration, strategic human resources, culture and leadership. Karen is a past executive member of the

Defence Women's Advisory Organization, a PhD candidate at the Royal Military College of Canada, and is continuously inspired by her 10-year old daughter Kelsy.

Dr. **Angela R. Febbraro** received her PhD in social psychology from the University of Guelph in 1998 and is currently a defence scientist at Defence Research and Development Canada – Toronto. She has published several articles on diversity in the Canadian Forces and has taught several courses in social and organizational psychology and in the psychology of gender.

Major (retired) **Sue Forgues** (Weicker) served as a tactical helicopter pilot in the Canadian Forces from 1988 – 2004. Her first operational tour was on the Twin Huey at 408 Squadron in Edmonton followed by an exchange tour with the Royal Air Force in the United Kingdom, flying the Puma. On her return to Canada, she was the Operations Officer at 403 Squadron in Gagetown and completed her career as Tactical Aviation Coordinator at 1 Canadian Air Division. Sue has written several magazine articles and appeared as a keynote speaker at the Canadian Defence Academy and Canadian Forces Leadership Institute *Women Leading in Defence* symposium in March 2006. Sue is married to Pierre Forgues and resides in Ottawa, Ontario.

Dr. **Irina Goldenberg** is a defence scientist at the Centre for Operational Research and Analysis within Defence Research and Development Canada. In her current posting within the Directorate of Human Rights and Diversity, Irina is responsible for conducting research on employment equity and gender integration issues within the Canadian Forces. Prior to her employment with the Department of National Defence, Irina worked within the Research Branch at the Correctional Service of Canada and taught in the Criminology Department at Carleton University.

A graduate of University of Western Ontario under the Medical Officer Training Plan, Commodore **Margaret Kavanagh** was posted to seven different geographical locations in Canada from Calgary, Alberta to Halifax, Nova Scotia, plus Lahr, Germany. She also served in Bahrain during the 1990 Persian Gulf Conflict. Her duties have included clinical general practice; operational medicine in the land, sea, and air environments; human physiological research following the completion of her Master's degree; and medical administration. She has functioned in the capacity of a senior physician in a clinic/hospital setting (Borden, Halifax and Lahr, Germany), as a staff officer in Headquarters (Trenton, Bahrain and Ottawa) and has command experience as the Commanding Officer of 1 Field Ambulance and 1 Canadian Field Hospital. Since 1998, she served in the Canadian Forces Health Services Group Headquarters in four different senior staff officer appointments and as the Deputy Commander for the Canadian Forces Health Services Group until her appointment as DGHS/Commander in April 2005. She is a graduate of the NATO Defence College and is a Certified Health Executive (CHE). She is an avid, semi-skilled golfer and partakes in a wide variety of sporting activities.

Major **Deanna Manson** of Cornwall, Ontario joined the Canadian Forces in 1989. She completed a Bachelor of Arts Degree in Honours History in 1993, and a Master of Arts Degree in Defence Management and Policy in 2005 at the Royal Military College of Canada in Kingston. An Air Force Logistics Officer by trade, she has enjoyed postings at Air Command Headquarters, Winnipeg; 14 Wing Greenwood; 1 Air Movements Squadron; and 1 Canadian Air Division Headquarters, Winnipeg. While posted to 1 Air Movements Squadron as a Mobile Air Movements Officer, she travelled extensively and participated in two international missions in 1998: the peacekeeping mission Op DETERMINATION (Kuwait) and the humanitarian mission Op CENTRAL (Honduras). Major Manson is currently with J3 Operations, Canadian Operational Support Command in Ottawa.

Lieutenant-Commander **Marta Mulkins** is a professional landscape architect and naval officer. She began her naval career in 1985 with HMCS *Donnacona* and has since served as a diesel mechanic and maritime surface officer with the Primary Reserve at HMCS *Carleton* and HMCS *York*; as the first Navigating Officer HMCS *Edmonton*; and as the Executive Officer HMCS *Summerside*. The first woman to be appointed to command a warship in the Canadian Navy, Lieutenant-Commander Mulkins assumed command of HMCS *Kingston* in 2003, followed by command of HMCS

Summerside in early 2005. Later that year, she returned to Ottawa to the Naval Strategic Communications Group, Chief of Maritime Staff at National Defence Headquarters, and in 2006 she deployed to Kabul, Afghanistan for a six-month tour in Operation ARGUS, the Canadian Forces' Strategic Advisory Team – Afghanistan. Lieutenant-Commander Mulkins holds an interdisciplinary Bachelor's Degree in (Industrial) Design and Environmental Studies from Carleton University, a Bachelor of Landscape Architecture from the University of Toronto, and is a graduate of the Joint Reserve Command and Staff College course at the Canadian Forces College. She is currently employed in Architecture and Engineering Resources with Public Works, Government Services Canada where she has been involved in a range of projects including a 2002 study of the security requirements of Parliament Hill, the Federal Judiciary and the National Archives. Lieutenant-Commander Mulkins is a member of the Ontario Association of Landscape Architects and the Canadian Society of Landscape Architects.

Major **Anne Reiffenstein** is the Chief Military Instructor at the Royal Military College of Canada, and as the Battle Commander of A Battery, 1 Canadian Mechanized Brigade Group from 2003–2005, she was the first woman to command a combat arms unit in Canada. She enrolled in the Canadian Forces in 1989 and was one of the first women to successfully complete artillery phase training in 1991. Major Reiffenstein is married to Major John Reiffenstein. They have two daughters – Grace who is seven, and Sadie who is five. Major Reiffenstein was a keynote speaker at the inaugural 2005 *Women Leading in Defence* symposium hosted by the Canadian Forces Leadership Institute, and was also a key contributor to the 2006 symposium.

Major **Jamie Speiser-Blanchet** is originally from Ottawa, Ontario and joined the Canadian Forces in 1990. After graduating from the Royal Military College in Kingston in 1994 with a Bachelor of Engineering in Computer Engineering, she went on to undertake her pilot training in Moose Jaw, Saskatchewan and Portage La Prairie, Manitoba. Upon receiving her Wings in March 1996, she was posted to 430e Escadron tactique d'hélicoptères (ETAH) at base des Forces canadiennes Valcartier, QC. During her 5 years at 430 ETAH, Major Speiser-Blanchet deployed on UN and NATO peacekeeping tours in Haiti (OP STABLE) and Bosnia (OP PALLADIUM), in addition to supporting such relief effort missions as Forest Fires in northern Québec, Saguenay Floods and the Ice Storm in Ontario and Québec. In 2001, Major Speiser-Blanchet was posted to 1 Wing Headquarters, Kingston, where she served as A3 Operations Task Officer, coordinating tactical aviation support and deployments for 1 Wing units across Canada. Posted to 403 (Helicopter) Operational Training Squadron, Gagetown, in 2003, she was employed as a line pilot and Aviation Tactics Flight Project Officer prior to her promotion to Major and subsequent appointment to her current position as Squadron Operations Officer. She is married to Capt Janin Blanchet, also a tactical aviation pilot with the Canadian Forces, and has two children, Emma and Zachary.

Index